Gramsci at Sea

Forerunners: Ideas First

Short books of thought-in-process scholarship, where intense analysis, questioning, and speculation take the lead

FROM THE UNIVERSITY OF MINNESOTA PRESS

Gregg Lambert
The World Is Gone: Philosophy in Light of the Pandemic

Grant Farred
Only a Black Athlete Can Save Us Now

Anna Watkins Fisher
Safety Orange

Heather Warren-Crow and Andrea Jonsson
Young-Girls in Echoland: #Theorizing Tiqqun

Joshua Schuster and Derek Woods
Calamity Theory: Three Critiques of Existential Risk

Daniel Bertrand Monk and Andrew Herscher
**The Global Shelter Imaginary: IKEA Humanitarianism
and Rightless Relief**

Catherine Liu
**Virtue Hoarders: The Case against the
Professional Managerial Class**

Christopher Schaberg
Grounded: Perpetual Flight . . . and Then the Pandemic

Marquis Bey
The Problem of the Negro as a Problem for Gender

Cristina Beltrán
**Cruelty as Citizenship: How Migrant Suffering
Sustains White Democracy**

Hil Malatino
Trans Care

Sarah Juliet Lauro
**Kill the Overseer! The Gamification of
Slave Resistance**

Alexis L. Boylan, Anna Mae Duane,
Michael Gill, and Barbara Gurr
**Furious Feminisms: Alternate Routes
on *Mad Max: Fury Road***

Ian G. R. Shaw and Marv Waterstone
**Wageless Life: A Manifesto for a Future
beyond Capitalism**

Claudia Milian
LatinX

(Continued on page 90)

Gramsci at Sea

Sharad Chari

University of Minnesota Press
MINNEAPOLIS
LONDON

ISBN 978-1-5179-1591-9 (PB)
ISBN 978-1-4529-6993-0 (Ebook)
ISBN 978-1-4529-7036-3 (Manifold)

Published by the University of Minnesota Press, 2023
111 Third Avenue South, Suite 290
Minneapolis, MN 55401-2520
www.upress.umn.edu

Available as a Manifold edition at manifold.umn.edu

Contents

Preface and Acknowledgments

> The shadow of tomorrow's impending ecological disaster leaps over today and reunites with abandoned conceptions of human finitude from a past rich with apocalyptic nightmares that the Enlightenment had temporarily vanquished.
>
> —SRINIVAS ARAVAMUDAN, *"The Catachronism of Climate Change"*

IN A LUCID CHARGE to critique our imperiled present in relation to prior forms of consciousness that also faced human finitude, Aravamudan diagnoses the past and present through a slow unfolding of a determinate future. This temporal structure offers no easy consolations of recuperating prior struggles, no reassurance that the negation of imperial catastrophe is forthcoming, and yet we witness the progressivist hopes bequeathed by the Enlightenment being inexorably undone.[1] I add that, in this process of slow decay, Enlightenment legacies reveal their contradictions well out into the horizon as we reach into dangerous waters of the near future to imagine what critique might yet be.

This cautiously recursive structure of thought encapsulates Antonio Gramsci's lifework, and in particular his political hope against the fascist high tide.[2] In a literal sense, the oceanic crisis of our time is planetary, just as the planetary crisis is oceanic, as it links crises bequeathed by waves of capital and imperialism. But these turgid conjunctures of socionatural disaster are also persistent well-

---

1. Adavamudan, "Catachronism," 8–9.
2. For a study of political hope in the remains of apartheid, Chari, *Apartheid Remains.*

springs of political hope against despair, despite their best attempts not to be. While Gramsci wrote little about the oceans, what he did write recasts his thought in useful ways. With oceanic archives and metaphors, we must therefore venture where no Gramscian has ventured before, remaining faithful to what he calls his philological method, betraying him properly when needs must.

My argument is that an *oceanic* reading of Gramsci, as a thinker of particular oceanic conjunctures but also as a thinker whose method is "oceanic," is precisely relevant to imperial extraction through the ocean and to the politics of representation in its wake. Gramsci, as is well recognized, helps us link the critique of capitalism and revolution with insurgent cultural forms in the hope of galvanizing collective political will. The claim in this little book is that he does so "oceanically," and that his thought can help our quest for post-terracentric explanation and representation as the world ocean warms.

I elaborate this argument in four moves. Chapter 1, "Gramsci and the Sea," explores what Gramsci has to say about the sea, and also how his leitmotifs or forms of thought can be read oceanically. The "Oceanic Question," chapter 2, picks up on Gramsci's "Notes on the Southern Question," read with contemporary work on oceanic capitalism, agrarian and Black Marxist traditions, and two neologisms: the activist category of "extractivism" and the industry category of "blue economy." The latter category boldly fetishize the fetishisms of capitalism, which takes us to waves of oceanic imperialism through Fernando Coronil's critique of Occidentalist forms of thought that divide the Northern (or terrestrial) Self from Southern (or oceanic) Other. Searching for a position beyond terracentrism, we might approach terraqueous articulations of land, labor, and capital through Karl Marx's critique of the fetishism of this "trinity formula." Coronil's reading of Marx, along with his critique of Occidentalism, points to terraqueous critique that refuses "Just One Last Watery Ghost-Dance" (chapter 3) of the reifications of *Monseiur le Capital* and *Madame la Terre*. The final chapter, "Storm," turns to Black Afrofuturist and aquafuturist artists, including the Drexciya collective, Ellen Gallagher, and John Akomfrah, read with Katherine McKittrick, and shows how waves of struggle continue to hold the possibility to "storm" us on different shores. Gramsci's materialist attention to the sublation—both cancelation and preservation—of prior struggles within hegemonic formations helps us see not just long genealogies of domination, but also of the persistence of the strike, abolition, internationalism, and emergent forms of anti-ecocidal struggle as holding the potential to storm contemporary terraqueous conjunctures. While such political storms are unpredictable and everywhere possible, Gramsci's caution to revolutionary internationalism is to contribute to the direction of their emergence. This Drexciyan Gramsci, from the ruins of "Americanism and Fordism," betrays the Sardinian properly, taking his thought to undercurrents necessary to will an actually different future into being.

The oceanic past is never past, but it will never return. We might take some solace in the conclusion of *Moby Dick,* in which the narrator floats in the aftermath of catastrophe in the coffin of the great harpooner and his erstwhile lover Queequeg, a coffin inscribed with the truths of Oceania that remain inscrutable to the narrator. In other words, Ishmael lives to tell the tale, but without the ability to comprehend, let alone claim, Indigenous knowledge in response to planetary crisis. Even that gesture remains ruined. Instead, as Gallagher and Charne Lavery remind us, it is Pip, the young Black cabin boy who is drowned but not quite saved, who can never unsee the madness in the ocean. Pip is the Gramscian organic intellectual of the oceanic crisis, the Drexciyan who refuses the second coming of a Marxish messiah but who faces the apocalyptic nightmares that return after the conclusive eclipse of the Enlightenment. And this is precisely the point at which the oceanic Gramsci returns to the radical traditions of the shipwreck, with Pip and political hope. A tragic scene, indeed. In our age of resurgence of deep socionatural forces, as centuries of oppression find new expressive articulation, scenes like these have the capacity to storm us in ways we cannot yet anticipate.

This book is experimental. I invite readers to dissent, to refuse anything and transform everything. I am grateful for the opportunity to have had brilliant interlocutors at the Summer School in Global Studies and Critical Theory on "the Sea" at the Academy of Global Humanities and Critical Theory, University of Bologna, in late June of 2022, with support for my participation from the Fondazione Gramsci Emilia-Romagna. I thank the brilliant seminar participants, as well as Sarah Nuttall, Ranjana Khanna, Sandro Mezzadra, Iain Chambers, Antonio Schiavulli, Achille Mbembe, Isabel Hofmeyr, Charne Lavery, Laleh Khalili, Gillian Hart, Matthew Shutzer, Rosanna Carver, Michael Watts, Philippe LeBillon, Alex Loftus, Jesse Rodenbiker, Asher Ghertner and participants at his graduate seminar at Rutgers, and an insightful referee. Samera Esmeir shared work in progress that influenced key arguments. Grant Farred offered the playful provocation that Gramsci is too important to be left to the Gramscians. Katherine McKittrick and Ellen Gallagher make Drexciyology and scrimshaw for us all. Leah Pennywark has been wonderfully supportive from our first interaction. Gratitude to the team at Minnesota, including Anne Carter and Mike Stoffel, for all that brings a little book into the world. Thanks to many colleagues and friends at Berkeley and at the Department of Geography, and also for a Humanities Research Fellowship and for a fellowship at the Stellenbosch Institute for Advanced Studies. Many friends across many seas offer all manner of support; I hope they see themselves between the lines. As always, thanks to Ma, Pa, Arvind, Jeannie, Nikhil, and Maya. Ismail remains my light and lifeboat.

1. Gramsci and the Sea

WHEN THE TWENTY-YEAR-OLD Antonio Gramsci left Ghilarza in October of 1911 on a journey *di là dale grandi acque* ("beyond the wide waters"), an expression that his biographer Giuseppe Fiori remarks could once be said without affectation, he did not yet know that he would begin a process of relentless questioning of his island's relationship to the peninsula, as well as a revision of his "Sardist" conception of the world.[1] His surviving school essay from his Sardinian youth, two editors argue, is "as vehement in his opposition to European imperialism in China as in his repetition of what (he recalled in 1924) was the favorite slogan of his schooldays: 'Throw the mainlanders into the sea!'"[2] There is more to these vignettes than an island country boy becoming Italian or internationalist. I suggest that that, even in these youthful gestures, there is an oceanic moment in Gramsci's thought, one open to the dividing sea that is nevertheless traversed in the hope of new and militant solidarities, one that recalls the colonial threat to drive the settler into the sea but remains dissatisfied with this simplification.

This is the topic of this first of four chapters through which I hope to arrive at a conceptualization of the oceanic question adequate to the present, with Gramsci as a proximal interlocutor. I argue that a

1. Fiori, *Antonio Gramsci,* 70.
2. Hoare and Nowell Smith, in Gramsci, *Selections from the Prison Notebooks,* xix.

submerged oceanic moment in Gramsci's thought enables a critique of the terracentric aims and metaphors of the Marxist tradition that Gramsci sought to renew in a moment of danger, a moment of danger that we of course face with differential intensities today. There is a tension in Gramsci's task in this regard. On the one hand, his literal reflections on the ocean concern a particular interimperial oceanics in which he notes the geopolitics and literary effects of shifting imperial fortunes. On the other hand, Gramsci's method contains an approach to multiple spatiotemporalities that is an important break from a stratigraphic form of thought in the Marxism of the Second International. Like Michel Foucault's genealogies, Gramsci's work points to long-term reconstitutions of power, and of the desire for it, while also cautiously holding to the possibility of revolutionary rupture with processes of political recuperation.

Taking a cue from Gramsci, we might follow oceanic leitmotifs in his method to think across his sea of notes: notes that might have been linked by hypertext in a different time. In so doing, we should keep in mind that Gramsci's method resists fixed definitions and static frameworks. His concepts are fluid and up for revision. He is relentlessly revisionist in his concept work and in his relational histories. Related to this is his philological method. Edward Said writes that, "despite his poverty and relatively humble origins, Gramsci was a disciplined philologist," implying that European linguistics was a rarefied, bourgeois, colonial tradition.[3] Gramsci subverted this tradition through his concern with *senso comune,* which he sought in forms like popular theater and serialized detective fiction. He would no doubt have joined us in two years of binging Netflix, particularly if it deepened his communist concern over the conditions for the production of militant consciousness. However, "leitmotif" as guiding principle—as in the recurring musical form in Wagner, or chords that signal the approach of Darth Vader or the shark in *Jaws*—is inadequate to Gramsci's attentiveness to the productivity

3. Said, "On Critical Consciousness," 24.

of cultural forms. Said emphasizes Gramsci's focus on "elaboration," *e-laborare* as refining or working-out, through which "culture itself or thought itself or art [becomes] a highly complex and quasi-autonomous extension of political reality" necessary to represent the hegemonic apparatus in order to dismantle it.[4] Gramsci's leitmotifs signal creative elaboration of concepts and histories. That is what he works on relentlessly. These are just some caveats.

I will make three moves here. I begin by reading what Gramsci wrote about the sea. I then note the figurative or metaphorical ways in which the oceanic enters his writing. I argue that Gramsci thinks in the key that Barbadian poet-historian Kwamu Brathwaite calls "tidalectictics," with its refusal of a terrestrial "obsession for fixity, assuredness and appropriation."[5] While Brathwaite does not pose his category to be thought dialectically, my suggestion is that he may have taken to Gramsci's earthy approach to dialectics. To make the case for a reading of Gramsci as an oceanic dialectician, we will have to think more about what he calls the "absolute earthliness and secularism of thought" as a response to the call to go below the waterline.[6] This will return us to the ensemble of Gramsci's concepts and to his living, pulsating archive of notes to think about the "oceanic feeling" that pervades them, in the hope that he would appreciate this appropriation of Romain Rolland's concept with the

4. Said, *World,* 170–71.

5. See DeLoughrey and Flores, "Submerged Bodies," for thoughtful elaboration on tidalectics as "submarine immersion and oceanic intimacy . . . constituted by an entangled ontology of diffraction" (138); Stephanie Hessler calls it "an oceanic worldview" and points to Brathwaite's discomfort with "dialectics" as a Western imposition. Thanks to Michael Cavuto for pushing me on this point; my response is that the gesture "not-West" is also a certain kind of dialectical gesture, that there are many approaches to dialectics, of which Gramsci's is heuristic and earthly, and that it is perhaps legible through Brathwaite's concerns with "riddims," flux, anger, myth, and hope.

6. Hofmeyr, *Dockside Reading,* 18; Rediker, "History from below the Water Line."

political hopes of an oceanic Marxist, a creature from the deep sea rather than the proverbial well-grubbed mole.

Gramsci on the Sea

The sea surfaces in an important way in Gramsci's political writings in 1924, a volatile year in his life. Gramsci had been in Moscow since May of 1922, and was not in Italy during the fascist assent to power and the arrests of communist leadership in 1923. In late 1923, he moved to Vienna, tasked with linking the Communist Party of Italy, formed with Amadeo Bordiga and others in 1921 in Livorno, with other communist parties. In February of 1924, he wrote to Palmiro Togliatti and Umberto Terracini in the leadership to argue that they had entered a new phase in the history of the party and the country, that they had to engage the Third International and also rethink their relationship to the masses, and then honed in on the "problem of the military fleet": "Italy lives from the sea; . . . to fail to concern oneself with the problem of the seamen, as one of the most important questions and worthy of the party's maximum attention would mean to not think concretely about revolution."[7]

One would think that such a strong statement would require elaboration, but it does not. I would like to think such a powerful statement is folded into other questions in his prison notebooks (*Quaderni del carcere*). Both propositions by the Sardinian are important and return in different forms in his writings: first, that Italy lives from the sea, and second, that seamen, particularly in the military fleet, are crucial to proletarian revolution.

In the early period of his incarceration, while he was shunted around prisons, Gramsci wrote in 1926 to his sister-in-law, Tatiana Schucht, about the penal island of Ustica: "You can't imagine how happy I am to wander from one corner of the island to another and

7. Gramsci, *Selections from Political Writings*, 202; Gramsci, *Antonio Gramsci Reader*, 134.

to breathe in the sea air after a whole month of being passed from one prison to another."[8] A letter meant for Piero Sraffa describes the arduous journey to Ustica, with seasickness in chains; a letter that never reached Schucht details another "rough crossing" from Ustica to Palermo and on to Naples in February of 1927.[9] He reflects from Milan that April in a letter to Schucht that in Ustica he "came to know a colony of Bedouins banished from Cyrenaica [Italian Libya] for political reasons," and that, in Naples, "I began to recognize a series of highly interesting types, whereas before the only southerners I had known at close quarters were Sardinians."[10] These letters offer an early revision and expansion of his statement on the importance of seamen. Perhaps, through this line of thought, Gramsci began to realize the limits to an anthropological rather than political conception of the subaltern. The embodied materiality of the sea is vividly present in seasickness and the brisk sea air, and in a structure of feeling that evokes the carceral sea as a contradictory space, a space of the emergence of new combinations in C. L. R. James *Mariners, Renegades and Castaways* and Peter Linebaugh and Marcus Rediker's *The Many-Headed Hydra*.

When he did start work in earnest on his notebooks, Gramsci was farthest from the phenomenal experience of the sea, but the materiality of the sea remained lodged in his consciousness as a precarious liminal zone. Gramsci does not name a sequence of notes on the sea directly, but certain themes emerge, beginning with Notebook 2, 1929–1933. He does not say it explicitly, but the concern across these notes is with a specific interwar ocean posed as a conjuncture in interimperial histories, with important cultural effects in the particular literary archives to which he had access.

In an extract from an article on the Italian merchant marine, Gramsci gets into the nitty gritty of wartime loss both for commerce and for the navy. He focuses in on the importance of freighters as

8. Gramsci, *Letters from Prison*, 62.

9. Gramsci, 67.

10. Gramsci, 83.

opposed to passenger liners during the war, which left a premium on liner building after the war, and drew capital to luxury steamliners precisely at a time of heightened mass migration; he also notes a tendency to gigantism and limits to the velocity of transoceanic circulation ("speed . . . must be held in check in order to be economical"); and he also notices that one can no longer think about the political economy of shipping in isolation from airspace.[11] In this note, Gramsci has an intuition about some of the key elements of transmodal logistics that would emerge only much later in the century, of the fantasy of smooth movement of commodities by land, sea, and air. He does not fetishize Marx's notion of the "annihilation of space by time," because it may not always make political-economic sense. He argues that technological change in the building of new kinds of ships lowers the value of previous ships destined for the ship-breaking yard; and he also notes that this dynamic forces people and goods into risky forms of shipping—risky both for seafarers and for the insurance industry, that is. Thinking in the aftermath of the First World War, Gramsci theorizes what Laleh Khalili calls the "sinews of war and trade," or the intertwining of military and capitalist dynamics.[12] By thinking across sea and air, he helps us ask how oceanic extraction in our time is linked in complex ways to the specter of outer-space mining as well.

Another sequence of notes concerns geopolitics. The first note in this sequence (Q2, §16) begins with a critique of an argument that "from the battle of Marathon until the world war, world politics have been controlled by Europe"; criticizing the ahistorical treatment of "the world," he adds sarcastically, "the Chinese and Indian

----

11. Q2, §12. Unless otherwise noted, all such references are to Gramsci, *Prison Notebooks,* and will be done in main text, with Q designating the original notebook number (for *Q* in the original title *Quaderni del carcere*), and § the note number within it. The International Gramsci Society's Concordance Tables help locate notes in English translation across anthologies; see internationalgramscisociety.org/resources/concordance_table/anthologies.html.

12. Laleh Khalili, *Sinews.*

civilizations must have counted for something." Then he turns to the history of the United States, and to the Washington conference of 1921–1922 that "dealt with China, with the balance of power in the seas of the Far East," while the Root–Takahira Agreement tried to stabilize relations with Japan. Gramsci notes the U.S. acquisition of the Philippines, Guam (from the Marianas), the Hawaiian Islands, and the Samoan island of Tutuila, and in the Caribbean Sea, U.S. power over Puerto Rico, leasing of Guantanamo Bay, control of customs at Haiti's Port-au-Prince, and financial and military power in the Dominican Republic. Gramsci is attentive to the diversity of political and economic arrangements in the terraqueous spread of U.S. power across oceans, and he would be engaged with Chinese geopolitics in the Indian and Pacific Oceans today.

Gramsci picks up on these themes in Q2, §40, on naval powers and Eurasian geopolitics from Scandinavia and the Baltic region to the possibility of a Russian-German bloc from the Arctic Sea to the Mediterranean, from the Rhine to the Pacific. He continues in §48, on "the constitution of the English Empire," with its combination of financial, industrial, and naval power. This attentiveness to the sinews of political-economic and military power becomes key to his reconceptualization of the notion of hegemony and, more precisely, of the integral state that conjoins civil and political hegemony. Scholars have tended to read Gramsci's thinking in a national and European frame, but in these notes, we see him thinking across oceans in an imperial frame. When he reflects on imperial geopolitics, there is a different quality to his spatial attentiveness as well: he notes that, although the Imperial Conference of 1926 defined different areas as "autonomous communities with equal rights," they in fact play differentiated roles in the imperial ensemble, also in control of the seas through the Indian and Australian navies. Then we have this enigmatic note §78, which I would like to read in full:

Atlantic-Pacific. The role of the Atlantic in modern culture and eco-nomics. Will this axis move to the Pacific? The largest masses of population in the world are in the Pacific: if China and India were to become modern nations with massive industrial production, their break from European dependence would really rupture the present balance—a transformation of the American continent, shifting the axis of American life from the Atlantic coast to the Pacific coast, etc. Examine all these questions in economic and political terms (trade, etc.)

If this sounds like conventional political science, we should keep in mind that Gramsci was mercilessly critical of the political science of his time. Just as Marx posed his task as a critique of political economy, Gramsci self-consciously engages across several notes in a critique of political science. We should instead keep in mind the notes I have suggested, in which imperial geopolitics are differentiated, and in which hegemony is an expansive and shifting geopolitical project in space and time. The concerns of these notes, however, do not seem to make explicit a spatial conception of imperial hegemony. His thoughts are very much part of what we can now see in retrospect as a set of late-imperial debates about oceanic power in the face of hegemonic continentalism, whether in the Pax Britannia, the Pax Americana, or the Third Reich.[13]

Consider note §97 of Q2, in which Gramsci interprets an anonymous article in his terms, as offering the hypothesis that the Unites States "wants to become the hegemonic political force of the British Empire, that is, it wants to conquer the English empire from within and not from the outside by war." This is quite a provocative interpretation of what would later be called the "special relationship" between the United States and Britain as actually a new way of becoming hegemonic; it is also an application of his own way of understanding the emergence of new hegemonic projects within the old, through the renovation of prior social institutions and power relations.

He picks up on this theme in Notebook 5 (1930–1932), §8, in a reading of Frisella Vella, whom he cites as proposing that, "since Asia is the most suitable area for American economic expansion,

13. Thanks to Matt Shutzer for this.

and since America's lines of communication with Asia go across the Pacific as well as across the Mediterranean, Europe must not oppose the transformation of the Mediterranean into a big artery of American-Asian commerce." Gramsci's own perspective is not always easy to discern in his readings of texts, except that he ends that Vella "is convinced of the inevitability of American global hegemony," while Gramsci never thinks hegemony is inevitable or unending. This note helps us see maritime sinews of empire as precisely the terrain of an ongoing and insecure imperial hegemony.

When Gramsci takes these insights out of a Eurocentric frame, he battles with his own limitations. That is the most generous way I can put it. In §23 of Q5, "Brief Notes on Chinese Culture. I," he argues that "England, America, and Japan . . . are superior to China not only 'militarily' but also economically and culturally; in short, they are superior in all areas of society." He continues: "Only the current 'cosmopolitan' unity of hundreds of millions of people with its specific form of nationalism based on 'race'—xenophobia—enables the central government of China to have at its disposal the minimal financial and military means with which to resist international pressures and keep its adversaries divided." Despite this insight, he reverts to Orientalism when he argues here: "One must not forget that the Chinese historical movement is confined to the Pacific coast and the banks of the great rivers that flow into the Pacific; the great mass of people in the hinterland is more or less passive." We ought to subject Gramsci to his own method here, to expect new forms of Chinese imperial power over land and sea; and we ought to insist on a critique of xenophobia and not simply an assertion of it, a point that the Sardinian had come to appreciate in his own critique of the Southern Question.

In Q5, §45, Gramsci just cites Enrico Catellani's article *"La libertà del mare."* He would have known Catellani's work a decade earlier on Germany's investment in the Luftwaffe as a means of gaining aerial military advantage over Britain's naval power. Recall he had already suggested that we think of the sea in relation not just to land but also to airspace (Q2, §12). He does not say more about the legal regimes that might govern the sea of the future, but we can surmise that he knew it would be important for the shift to American imperial hegemony.

The next note on "naval issues" is §60 in Q6, which turns to the relative visibility of naval as opposed to landed armaments: "Naval armaments are hard to conceal; it is impossible to have secret ship-yards or cruisers built in secret." He then compares England as an island reliant on its connections with its colonies "to provision its populations, whereas America is a self-sufficient continent, has two oceans that are connected by the Panama Canal." He then asks: "Why should a state relinquish its geographic and strategic advan-tages if these put it in a position conducive to world hegemony? Why should England have a certain hegemony over a set of countries based on certain traditional conditions that favored its superiority, if the United States can be superior to England and absorb it, together with its empire, if possible?" This is back to the "special relation-ship"; an editor's note to §60 argues we should read this in light of the Washington Naval Conference of 1921–1922, which included a treaty between Britain and the United States to maintain parity in naval power (see Q2, §97).

While Gramsci is absorbed in these intrigues over world hege-mony, he also asks other questions about them. For instance, in Q8, §124, on "the economic corporative phase of Italian history, the Lepanto enterprise," shifts the debate about the naval battle at Lepanto to note that, "of the more than two hundred ships that took part in the battle, only fourteen were Spanish; all the others were Italian," and he critiques an account that makes a claim that there was no part of the peninsula that did not take part in Lepanto. Gramsci questions the methodological nationalism of this account and asks for more intricate accounting of the political and economic arrangements through which "soldiers from diverse regions of Italy [were] enrolled" in inter-imperial war.

There is another linked but quite different theme across anoth-er set of notes that are broadly on the cultural effects of oceanic geopolitics, and more particularly on ways of dealing with the end of naval or commercial power. In Notebook 3, §78, one of several notes about conservative populist writing called "Father Bresciani's progeny," turns to the popular serial novel, reading in Jules Verne "anti-English sentiment, linked to the loss of colonies and to the lingering pain of naval defeats." Gramsci has something of the book historian in him as well. In Q4, §93 ("Intellectuals. Brief Notes on English Culture"), he argues not just that "the loss of naval and trade supremacy" has effects for content, but that the commerce in "American books, together with American culture, . . . are an increasingly competitive threat to English books." The entire process of publishing, distribution, and advertising, he thinks, is becoming more American. And this is an effect of the oceanic geopolitical shifts in the Anglosphere.

This is what Gramsci has to say explicitly about oceanic matters, but there is more to be said about the oceanic metaphors that pervade his notes. In Q2, §32, Gramsci reads an anonymous text and speculates that the author is a Russian exile with ties with the English right wing committed to the notion of an inevitable Anglo–Russian war. He concludes: "Official relations between the two countries resemble the waves on the surface of the ocean which come and go capriciously; but deep down there is the strong historical current which leads to war." What do we make of these metaphors of surface waves and deep currents?

Gramscian Tidalectics

The language of currents recurs across the notes: currents of thought, socialist currents, literary currents, philosophical currents, non-Marxist currents, cultural currents, ideological currents, political currents, currents of public opinion, currents of popular passion, main currents, continental currents, religious-ecclesiastical currents, optimistic currents, modern currents, individual currents, Italian currents, Jacobin currents, and less vulgar currents. And that's just in Notebook 1. On the other hand, there are waves of revolutionary activity, waves of literary experimentation, waves of workers movements, waves of anticlericism, waves of insurrection that are not revolutionary, and those that are. The wildly inconsistent use of these metaphors means they were not meant to be concepts.

How, then, do we make sense of the statement that "waves on the surface come and go capriciously, but deep down there is the strong historical current"? How do we read this with Gramsci's relentless intention to break with mechanistic materialism in the Marxist tradition? As various readers of Gramsci note, he takes as axiomatic across several of his notes this passage from Marx's 1859 preface to the *Critique of Political Economy*:

> No social order ever perishes before all the productive forces for which there is room in it have developed; and new, higher relations of production never appear before the material conditions for their existence have matured in the womb of the old society. Therefore, mankind always sets itself only such tasks as it can solve; since, looking at the matter more closely, it will always be found that the task itself arises only when the material conditions for its solution already exist or are at least in the process of formation.[14]

The first statement is a refutation of a stageist conception of modes of production. The old social order (capitalism) cannot die while its technologies have room or scope; and yet the new (let us call it *X*, as Kojin Karatani does) cannot yet appear.[15] The second statement is about the "problem space," to use David Scott's term, that Gramsci is always in.[16] The task that mankind sets itself can appear only when the solution is already in formation. This does not mean it is inevitable, or we would know what to do with fossil-fuel capital; but we might know what is to be done in theory.

As we return to the metaphors of waves and deep currents, we should note that Gramsci himself argues that a concept-metaphor emerges from and should be understood in relation to "the histor-

14. Marx, "Preface."
15. See Karatani and Wainwright, "Critique."
16. Hall, "David Scott."

ically determined cultural world from which it sprang."[17] This is a precise corollary to the passage from Marx above that Gramsci takes as axiomatic, and its implication is that there is more to Gramsci's oceanic metaphors than meet the eye.

I have suggested that the statement on currents and waves in §32 of Q2 expresses Gramsci's own attempt to think in a nonmechanistic way about the relation between structure and superstructure. So let us turn to a key note on the relation between structure and super-structure, §17 in Q13. "In studying structure," Gramsci writes in this note, "it is necessary to distinguish organic movements (relatively permanent) from movements which may be termed 'conjunctural' (and which appear as occasional, immediate, almost accidental)."[18] Conjunctural phenomena "give rise to political criticism of a minor, day to day character"; on the other hand, "organic phenomena give rise to socio-historical criticism." On the face of it, this seems to be a theorization of the metaphor of surface waves and deep currents. In periods of protracted crisis, Gramsci continues, organic contra-dictions become apparent on the terrain of the conjunctural—that is, on the surface. The problem Gramsci identifies here is that critics tend to approach this eruption of the organic into the conjunctural through either "an excess of 'economism,'" or "an excess of ide-ologism" when the challenge is in apprehending "the dialectical nexus between the two categories of movement, and therefore of research," and he adds: "If error is serious in historiography, it be-comes still more serious in the art of politics."[19]

As a methodological operation, for research and for politics, Gramsci proposes in this note that we distinguish three "moments or levels": first, the "relation of social forces which is closely related to the structure . . . and which can be measured with the systems of the exact or physical sciences;" second, "the relation of political forces," which is also the terrain of "self-awareness" and of the

17. Q11, §50, cited in Morton, "Traveling with Gramsci," 48.
18. Gramsci, *Selections from the Prison Notebooks,* 177.
19. Gramsci, 178.

formation of collective political consciousness and organization; and third, "the relation of military forces which from time to time is directly decisive."

What Gramsci does not intend by the metaphor of "levels" is a Marxist stratigraphy in which the deeper level offers truths about higher levels. Note 17 of Q13 warns against thinking of these moments or levels in these causal terms. There is no inevitable "process of development from one moment to the next;" instead, he concludes, "contradictory outcomes are possible: either the old society resists and ensures itself a breathing-space, by physically exterminating the élite of the rival class and terrorizing its mass reserves; or a reciprocal destruction of the conflicting forces occurs, and a peace of the graveyard is established, perhaps even under the surveillance of a foreign guard."[20] I will return to this final phrase.

What I am calling Gramsci's "tidalectics" is in fact pitted against a stratigraphic way of thinking; it is also a dialectical method key to thinking about oceanic processes in the wake of a patriarch of oceanic studies, Fernand Braudel, and his ambitious and deliberate layering of geographical histories of the Mediterranean, in which the deepest layer of oceanic history is "organic" in a different way, as the environment is a shaping force but not one that erupts into the conjunctural surface in quite the same way as in Gramsci's imagination.[21] Much has been written about thinking beyond the waning light of Braudel's *Mediterranean* volumes, but it is his structure of thought, with its deep environmental determinism, that remains so powerful. Gramsci's dialectical method offers something very different; it pushes against landed and layered grammars of historical temporalization.[22]

Crucial to this project is Gramsci's hope that organic contradictions can be discerned on the terrain of the conjunctural to shape political and military strategy; this is all the more important when,

---

20. Gramsci, 185
21. Braudel, *The Mediterranean*.
22. Thanks, again, to Matt Shutzer.

as Gramsci claims through Marx, the material conditions for the new (X) are in the process of their materialization in the world and in theory, and just as importantly when they are not. To exemplify the latter, Gramsci turns to the exhaustion of a particular under-standing of revolution in Europe in the late nineteenth century: the notion of "permanent revolution" and the emergence, he elaborates in other notes, of what he calls "passive revolution."

I should pause to say that there is a great deal of debate about the concept of "passive revolution." Anglophone writers have tend-ed to fix the concept in ways that a more careful and philological reading across Gramsci's notes cannot sustain. Philological reading became possible with Valentino Gerratana's 1975 critical edition of the *Prison Notebooks,* only some of which have been translated into English by Joseph Buttigieg since the 1990s. Peter Thomas is in-dispensable in the Anglophone work, and he argues that we should think of passive revolution as a heuristic formula that allows for different formulations in different contexts, even though it emerged from debates in 1920s communism about how to think about "the revolution in permanence" in the politically fraught interwar peri-od.[23] It is also a framework for thinking with the axiomatic passage from Marx's 1859 preface in a practice of "political and strategic reflection," which for him in 1930s Italy required an engagement with Benedetto Croce, Machiavelli, and Marx.[24]

In elaborating this argument, Gramsci turns, as he often does, to a very schematic treatment of complex histories, as he writes in shorthand that the foreclosure of the French Revolution meant that, over a sequence of convulsions, the spirit of Jacobinism was sub-lated in a new form of political power that, by the end of the nine-teenth century, restored hegemony by reviving older political and economic forms. This was not just the fate of revolution in France; it was also, in a different way, the fate of Italian unification and its

23. Thomas, "Gramsci's Revolutions," 123.
24. Thomas, 124.

restoration of mercantile and landed power. Gramsci is extremely careful about the spatial differentiation of passive revolution in various forms, even while he is extremely schematic. In different ways, passive revolution conserves the old, it hijacks the language of revolution that Gramsci in an important note calls "revolution-restoration" or "revolution without revolution" (Q1, §44).[25]

If we turn to the ensemble of concepts that Gramsci works with "philologically," what is striking is that passive revolution leads him to continue to labor on his to-his-mind-incomplete 1926 piece titled "Some Aspects of the Southern question." Written before his imprisonment, the 1926 piece was Gramsci's reckoning with the social origins of the Sardist ideology of his childhood, as well as a schematic mapping of the conditions for a recasting of the "Southern Question" to enable the political alliance of northern workers and southern peasants under the leadership of an emerging proletarian hegemony in Turin and Milan. The incarcerated Gramsci turned to the heuristic of passive revolution in different ways to reckon with the defeat of this worker-led communist hegemony, or the transformations of the hegemonic apparatus in various ways in various times.

And as he works on passive revolution through his prison notes, it appears to be a form of "political and strategic reflection" in the wake of multiple defeats: at some points it is about explaining the failed possibilities of the Italian Risorgimiento; at others the sublation of "the revolution in permanence" in Europe, including, as we see in his letters on the centralization of power under Stalin, after the Russian Revolution; and it is a reckoning with the defeats of revolutionary currents from the French Revolution across the nineteenth-century landscape. At every moment, Gramsci is interested in what is nascent in these moments of defeat, to imagine their end. It is not surprising that this framework has been fruitful for thinkers in the later twentieth century and early twenty-first

25. See Morton, "Traveling with Gramsci," 55.

century concerned with the degradation of anticolonial nationalism, as in the work of Frantz Fanon, Partha Chatterjee, Stuart Hall,
Gillian Hart, and others.[26]

We ought to pause to do what Gramsci suggests, to notice the
rhythm of a thinkers thought. Within the ensemble of his concepts,
passive revolution is central to his critique of political science, and
to the rethinking of the notion of uneven and combined development of capitalism without the mechanistic materialism, economism, or voluntarism in various strands of radical thought. As
Gramsci elaborates over a series of notes on passive revolution, he
is not interested only in the residues of "historical Jacobinism" in
the unmaking of the French Revolution, but also in the sublation,
as both cancelling and preserving what he calls a Jacobin spirit
in the political formation to come. Hence, the revolutionary eighteenth century gave way to a series of struggles in the nineteenth
century that, by the 1870s, both cancelled and preserved the spirit
of Jacobinism in a new kind of hegemony that made claims to the
past while ensuring a break with popular militancy. Gramsci's notes
might seem to exemplify these shifts within a European frame, but
his notes on the sea point to what it might mean to think of them
in an imperial frame.

The key point I would like to make here is that the rhythm of
Gramsci's thought, and particularly his wrestling with a materialist
conception of sublation, gives more than metaphoric significance
to his notion of waves and currents. His note on structure and superstructure, §17 of Q13, conveys a nonmechanistic and nonidealist
notion of sublation and actualization, a particular kind of "tidalictic"
approach that avoids both mechanistic materialism and idealist voluntarism. Sublation of the spirit of Jacobinism points to submerged
legacies of popular struggle that might surface at various opportune
moments. I have suggested a particular reading of Gramsci, that

26. Fanon, *Wretched of the Earth*; Chatterjee, *Nationalist Thought and
the Colonial World*; Hall, *Hard Road*; Hart, *Rethinking the South African Crisis*.

the sea was for him not just an abstraction, but part of a tidalectical method that pushes well beyond the limits of a stratigraphic and terracentric imagination. That is his oceanic method.

Gramsci's Oceanic Marxism

From the early sketch of "Some Aspects of the Southern Question" to his subsequent elaborations on passive revolution, the making and unmaking of the "hegemonic apparatus," the intellectual, and the articulation of subaltern political will, Gramsci keeps returning to the unanswered questions of his youth. How do we understand the subordination of the south, and of Sardinia and particular, if not by driving the settler into the sea? I have suggested that the recursive quality of Gramsci's thought, his reading of the cancelation and preservation of prior struggles in new hegemonic formations, reflects what he suggests is a relation between, on the one hand, the conjunctural surface as waves rocking the boat of prisoners to the penal isle of Ustica, and on the other, the deep currents that sometimes break into that surface, including the surface of militant consciousness.

So, what might we make of Gramsci's "oceanic feeling," a phrase from Romain Rolland that he would undoubtedly have labored with. Rolland referred to what he thought was a religious experience, a feeling of oneness with everything that he had discerned in the Indian mystics Ramakrishna and Vivekananda. Freud, his interlocutor, shared Rolland's sense of despair with the West in a time of World War, but he mobilized Rolland's concept differently. Ranjana Khanna argues that, in *Civilisation and Its Discontents,* "Freud set up the modern ego against something named the *oceanic feeling*" not in Rolland's sense but "as a regression to primary narcissism."[27] Gramsci was certainly as interested as Rolland in the importance of forging a "conception of the world" different from but nonconflictual with that held by the West. Yet, neither Rolland's spiritu-

27. Khanna, *Dark Continents,* 90–93.

alism nor Freud's particular psychoanalytic response would have been adequate to Gramsci's "absolute secularization and earthliness of thought" (Q11, §27). He does not exactly elaborate on what he means by this phrase, although we know from the rhythms of his thought that it would require interrogating not only the Christian foundations of European secularism and the colonial foundations of Roland's orientalism, but also, as Isabel Hofmeyr puts it, the oceanic "spiritscapes" that persist despite "hydrocolonialism."[28] Gramsci's oceanic feeling would also have to historicize the European oceanic sublime in the shipwrecks of J. M. W. Turner or the great white whale of Herman Melville's *Moby Dick*.[29] Gramsci would have to elaborate Rolland's concept through attention to multiple imaginaries and to the materiality of the sea.

If there is an oceanic Marxism in Gramsci, a Marxist engaged with the ocean as we see it today, it would have to attend to two things. First, this oceanic Gramsci would have to stretch his notion of the "organic," which may have entered his thought through Henri Bergson, to take this speculative concept back through "the earthliness of thought."[30] Gramsci's *organicitá* might have taken him to deepen a conception of biopolitics, particularly as the passive revolution across imperial space forged a terraqueous infrastructure in defense of some forms of life, and not others. This might have taken him to the world ocean transformed into our contradictory ocean, with its own "peace of the graveyard . . . perhaps even under the surveillance of a foreign guard" (Q2, §17).[31]

Second, we might keep in mind the letter Gramsci wrote to his son Delio in 1932:

Dearest Delio, I heard you went to the sea and saw some very beautiful things. I'd like you to write me a letter describing these beauties. Did you discover some new living creature? There's so much teem-

28. Hofmeyr, *Dockside Reading,* 37.
29. Corbin, *Lure of the Sea.*
30. Thanks to Jake Orbison for this insight.
31. Gramsci, *Selections from the Prison Notebooks,* 185.

ing life near the sea: little crabs, medusas, starfish, etc. A long time ago, I promised to write you some stories about the animals I used to know as a boy, but then I wasn't able to do so. Now I'll try to tell you one or two.[32]

In this letter to his young son, we see Gramsci's journey from his own childhood in Sardinia, from the notion of driving the settlers into the sea to remembering the teeming life of the sea. In this child's eye view, a different but still embodied and earthly political horizon emerges, one of radical kinship with "little crabs, medusas, starfish, etc." What might it mean to constitute collective political will to refuse its transformation into a graveyard as well?

32. Gramsci, *Letters from Prison*, 247.

2. The Oceanic Question

THE DEEP SEA, at depths greater than two hundred meters, is an expanse of 360 square kilometers; it is about half the planet's surface, and 95 percent of the Earth's biosphere. From the diversity of bioluminescent life, to mineral-rich polymetallic nodules, to chemosynthetic life next to hydrothermal vents, the deep ocean is an environment so alien to humans that its biology is "astrobiology": life forms that may be more like those on other planets than the proverbial E.T. Much of the deep sea remains unknown and understudied. We cannot know how anthropogenic change impacts the Greenland shark, the longest living vertebrate, with a lifespan of 392 years (plus or minus 120), or the black coral near the Azores, with its lifespan of 2,320 years (plus or minus 90), or the ten-mile-long sea-grass meadow off the coast of Spain, the oldest known single organism on the planet. Most of the deep sea is beyond the regulatory reach of individual states: 64 percent of the high sea is beyond national "exclusive economic zones" (EEZs), about 1.2 percent is protected. To put it differently, "oceanic feeling" in the literal sense is a pipe dream.

Demand for minerals and metals particularly in "tech" has intensified interest in deep-sea minerals, including polymetallic sulfides around hydrothermal vents, cobalt-rich crusts (CRCs) along seamounts, and fields of manganese polymetallic nodules on abyssal plains. The sea bed contains high-value ores like gold, silver, and platinum, but it is copper, nickel, cobalt, and rare earth elements that are sought for electronic devices and for batteries in wind turbines, solar panels, electric cars, and other elements of a low-carbon energy transition. There is no way to extricate these resources from being deeply intertwined with ecologies, often including unique habitats of marine species. These are deeply intertwined oceanic assemblages. Many of these oceanic environs are recognized as vulnerable marine ecosystems (VMEs), but the International Seabed Authority (ISA) tasked with regulating the deep-sea floor appears to be primarily a handmaiden to deepened exploitation. As of late August 2022, attempts to forge a U.N. ocean treaty had not yet come to fruition, and precious time continues to be lost.[1]

For corporations as well, deep-sea mining is risky and extremely expensive. Canadian Nautilus Minerals Incorporated filed for insolvency in 2019 just before it was meant to mine near Papua New Guinea; AngloAmerican divested from Nautilus the year before; many of the senior staff at Nautilus moved to Deep Green Metals to continue the work. The U.S. weapons corporation Lockheed Martin has been exploring seabed minerals through U.K. Seabed Resources with strong support from senior members of the British government, while the same government promotes a "blue belt" of protected marine areas. The European Commission poses deep-sea mining as conducive to "blue growth." The language of "blue economy" and "blue growth" makes explicit the contradictory environmentalization of deep-sea mining. Gerard Barron, CEO of DeepGreen, says: "At DeepGreen, we don't think of ourselves as developing a mining business. We are in the transition business—we

1. Kathryn Miller. Kirsten Thompson, Paul Johnston, and David Santillo, et al., "An Overview of Seabed Mining of Seabed Mining Including the Current State of Development, Environmental Impacts, and Knowledge Gaps," Frontiers in Science, January 10, 2018, frontiersin.org/articles/10 .3389/fmars.2017.00418/full; Greenpeace, *In Deep Water*; Hannah Moore with Jonathan Watts, "The Race to Mine the Deep Sea," March 27, 2022, in *Seascape: The State of Our Oceans,* produced by Courtney Yusuf and Rudi Zygadlo, podcast, MP3 audio, 32:12, theguardian.com/news/audio/2022 /mar/28/the-race-to-mine-the-deep-sea-today-in-focus-podcast.

want to help the world transition away from fossil fuels with the smallest possible climate change and environmental impact." Mike Johnson, former CEO of Nautilus adds that the seafloor promises "metals essential for the green economy."

Deep-sea mining is only one part of this blue economy, apparently key to our low-carbon future. I have suggested that the emergence of the blue economy as object is a window into the environmental-ization of the ocean at a time of intensified plunder and pollution. Picking up from the last chapter, Gramsci's oceanic Marxism recasts this contradictory object as a new twist in planetary passive revolu-tion, a revolution of capital in blue-green environmental garb that offers a political, economic, and ideological reshaping of the vast majority of our planet that remains outside our understanding or control, to turn it into a frontier for corporate plunder in the name of the planet and its denizens. Paraphrasing Ruthie Gilmore, this is another case of using capital to save capital from capital, with the life of the planet as a small price to pay. The virtue of Gramsci's method is that it allows us to think of different routes into this problematic, to avoid the lure of a generic, undifferentiated, and speculative formulation. As a heuristic, passive revolution prompts us to explore space-times of power and resistance as accumulative. Critique of the blue economy would have to ask how this object of speculation is deployed in concrete instantiations of a planetary passive revolution. That is the approach of an oceanic Gramsci.

I begin this exploration of the oceanic question with an important book on the political economy of capitalism and the sea, read in counterpoint to the legacy behind Gramsci's "Southern Question," which was the basis of his many years of study of passive revolution. The legacy from which Gramsci draws, somewhat lightly, is the classical Marxist "agrarian question." I will then turn to recent work on "extractivism," to argue that approaches to extractive industry from agrarian studies are particularly suited to extending Gramsci's approach. I will conclude with what this means for a conception of oceanic capitalism attentive to deep-sea mining and other forms of oceanic extraction. This will take us to the third chapter, which explores the other aspect of Gramsci's notion of passive revolution, which is its focus on waves of imperial power that have shaped the deep ocean as a tabula rasa for corporate plunder. In the final chapter, we turn to traditions and imaginations of resistance to this inevitability.

"Some Aspects of the Southern Question" was Gramsci's initial attempt at mapping out the material and ideological elements that kept the South, and his native Sardinia, in a state of social domination. Early in this unfinished piece, Gramsci writes that, in order for the northern proletariat to become directive of an anticapitalist alliance of classes, it has to gain the consent of the peasantry. Then he pauses and says he does not mean the "peasant and agrarian question in general," but rather as historically produced through the Southern Question and the Vatican. Gramsci does not, to my reading, return to what the agrarian question meant to its classical Marxist progenitors, Vladimir Lenin and Karl Kautsky among them. There is some debate about what of Lenin Gramsci had access to in order to read as carefully as he did, given his philological acuity, since very little was published in Italian and he had only some French newspaper sources, but given his emphasis on close readings of specific passages in Marx, it is significant that the agrarian question does not return as a significant problematic in his prison notes.[2]

In the 1970s and 1980s revival of agrarian studies, a new generation of agrarian Marxists returned to the classical agrarian question for an interpretation of agrarian capitalism as differentiated, shaped in different ways by the material and ecological conditions of agriculture. The agrarians' attentiveness to diverse configurations of land, labor, and capital prefigured a critique of capitalism attentive to racial/sexual difference at the level of households. Moreover, agrarian Marxism was committed to anticolonial, peasant, and proletarian struggles and their consequences. Since the 1980s, this agrarian tradition has produced important studies of

2. Davidson, "Gramsci and Lenin."

capitalist social transformation in which environmental and social differentiation was central. In the main, agrarian Marxists attended to spatial difference through the metaphor of national or regional "roads" or "paths," to think across comparative histories. Geographical metaphors of roads, paths, or trajectories shaped the spatiotemporal methods in this tradition, despite the intentions of thinkers attentive to the interaction of multiple histories and spatial processes to break from a positivist conception of path dependency. My own research in South India and South Africa has tried in different ways to deal with the ways in which the past shapes the present in nonlinear and nonteleological ways. The opportunity of thinking the agrarian question in the sea offers another iteration of this problem. I offer a close reading of Liam Campling and Alejandro Colás's *Capitalism and the Sea,* noting at the outset that Campling is a scholar rooted in Marxist agrarian studies, and an editor of a key journal in this field.

Capitalism and the Sea

Campling and Colás begin by posing a "terraqueous predicament": while capitalism aims to subsume the planet and its life forms, it "regularly confronts geophysical barriers to its own self-expansion, which in the case of the sea are especially challenging," because "the high seas cannot be permanently occupied."[3] This is in some ways a restatement of the classical agrarian question, which explains the unevenness and differentiation of agrarian capitalism as a consequence of agrarian ecological and social difference. What makes capital's encounter with the sea different is that, in its quest for a "spatial fix" to its immanent contradictions, it is forced to forge "new articulations of terraqueous territoriality" or "uniquely capitalist alignments of sovereignty, exploitation and appropriation

3. Campling and Colás, *Capitalism and the Sea,* 2.

in the capture and coding of maritime spaces and resources."[4] This is how they set up the problematic of oceanic capitalism.

One of the things that happens in oceanic books is that they can mirror the expansiveness of their object of study, and hence the adjective "Braudelian." I cannot rehearse all that Campling and Colás do. What I can do is draw out some key threads that might help us think about the oceanic question as the agrarian question at sea: as concerned with how capital creates "terraqueous territorialities" in relation to the challenges of marine environments. I read the book for moments in which we see oceans as produced through various conjunctures, as an oceanic Gramsci might, as products of different configurations of capital, law, labor, geopolitics, and technology, and importantly, of the natural qualities of the ocean that humans have apprehended as a source of energy, as protein for consumption or energy for propulsion.[5] Through attention to these organic qualities, the oceanic question is analogous to the classical agrarian question but with its distinctiveness. The ocean's specificity as an organic space of a different kind from farms, pastures, or forests is that it cannot be similarly "improved." There are limits to an oceanic green revolution, despite sea-cucumber farming, or Japanese high-value tuna ranching, or experiments in deep-sea mineral seeding. Rather, capital has to find different ways of extracting value from highly migratory species through rent extraction from national-territorial EEZ waters or from fishing quotas. We will return to the importance of rent in oceanic extraction.

Capital, state, and multilateral agencies come together to appropriate value from parcels of marine biomass that are in fact value in motion. The same principle applies to the extraction of value through oceanic shipping, still the cheapest means of enabling massive flows of goods in our time. But the lively unpredictability of the ocean consistently thwarts the fantasy of frictionless move-

4. Campling and Colás, 3.
5. Campling and Colás, 12.

ment across and through the seas, as witnessed in the periodicity of oceanic accidents and spills and in containers thrown overboard through storms and accidents.

The materiality of the ocean means that every new form of oceanic extraction—of deep-sea minerals, wave energy, desalinized water, or oceanic cooling systems using temperature differentials of surface and deep waters—comes at such great cost because of the added expense of legal, administrative, and military power needed to bring order to the sea. This means that hegemonic powers benefit most, and a key though not uncontested beneficiary has been American naval and commercial hegemony over the seas since 1945, the specific oceanic hegemony whose emergence Gramsci was concerned with. As a consequence, a "global commons," meaning the high seas beyond any nation's territorial waters, appears to privilege hegemonic corporate and state powers that seem to order and protect these interests through a naval, communication, energy, and financial infrastructure bequeathed by prior sinews of imperial power, to draw from Laleh Khalili's framing.[6]

Part of the oceanic question has to attend to the way in which the United Nations Convention on the Law of the Sea (UNCLOS) in 1982 effectively enclosed the oceans. Campling and Colás call this "the largest enclosures in human history" that used national-territorial EEZs to turn coastal terraqueous space into state property, and that made the high seas a "global commons" or "heritage of humankind" supposedly beyond reach of sovereignty and property.[7] These zones recall a relation between the notion of the "free sea" from Hugo Grotius's 1609 *Mare liberum* and the "closed sea" in John Selden's 1618 *Mare clausum,* as well as Western legal concepts of *imperium* or sovereignty and *dominium* or property over maritime space, conceptions that have recurred in histories of the seas ever since. We return to these imperial dynamics in the next

6. Campling and Colás, 13–14; Khalili, *Sinews.*
7. Campling and Colás, *Capitalism and the Sea,* 68–69.

chapter. The U.N. convention has to be seen in light of histories of imperialism and decolonization in and through the oceans, as we will see in chapter 4.

Another aspect of the "agrarian question at sea" is the ceaseless production of a diversity of labor regimes, rather than a march of proletarianization. This was one of the great insights of the agrarian Marxist tradition: it demonstrated painstakingly the diversity of arrangements of land, labor, and credit, and the nonlinearity of forms of tied or unfree labor even in dynamic regions of agrarian capitalism. Intense exploitation and persisting forms of unfreedom including debt bondage and slave labor have had extremely nonlinear histories in the oceans, and they persist into today's hidden oceanic labor regimes, including in twenty-first-century forms of slavery and indenture. Campling and Colás make a stronger argument that "people labouring at sea in the early twenty-first century remain crucial to keeping capitalism global; . . . their work makes possible the fragmentation of production and labour arbitrage across the planet."[8] Differentiated and highly exploitative labor at sea enables the arbitrage at the heart of global inequality, as it connects the unequal diversity of labor regimes across global capitalism today. This is also an interesting point because maritime labor has also been a conduit of resistance to various moments of power and inequality. The agrarian question at sea also has to attend to attempts to discipline these potentials for resistance as well.

One aspect of disciplining maritime labor regimes is that international labor law and trade unionism have tended to distinguish and deal separately with seafarers and fishing crews. Another set of issues emerge from the articulation of labor regimes across land and sea. All maritime labor regimes are in fact terraqueous: they begin with onshore recruitment, and higher levels of exploitation are enabled by "flags of convenience," the registration of ships in locations with weaker labor and environmental protections. G. Balachandran,

8. Campling and Colás, 109.

indispensable Indian Ocean labor historian, shows that by the mid-nineteenth to the early twentieth centuries, the constant churn in the maritime labor market was linked to agrarian landscapes through a range of intermediaries.[9] Political and economic subordination of agrarian households has been key to sustaining cheap maritime labor regimes in the past and present. And if the maritime workforce has historically appeared to be male dominated, still the larger terraqueous landscape of labor has continued to rely on a range of gendered forms of unpaid reproductive and productive labor, including of course hidden domestic- and community-care work. Linebaugh and Rediker present this argument particularly on the making of the Atlantic as a racial capitalist ocean, but it holds across oceanic conjunctures.

Ships are also labor regimes unto themselves. Rediker's history of slave ships carefully details the way in which they were also despotic factories meant to produce the commodity "labor" through systematic terror while also exploiting seafarers, but slave ships also enabled new and enduring forms of solidarity below deck.[10] Stephanie Smallwood's *Saltwater Slavery* shows that there is more than simply the transatlantic slave trade being the rational machine we see through the archives of slavery: for slaves, the process of commodification was violent in its indeterminacy, and this violence persisted in the "serial repetition of one-way departures" as "saltwater slaves" kept arriving on American shores. These accounts can be read in dialectical relation to think about the indeterminacy of all forms terraqueous labor, and also of possibilities of solidarity in the face of pervasive indeterminacy and violence.

Apart from the exploitation of human labor is the massive extraction of marine life through a fishing industry that has increasingly eroded the fisheries it relies on. Capital's response has been through new technologies for extraction from untapped frontiers

9. Balachandran, *Globalizing Labour?*
10. Rediker, *Slave Ship.*

or for removing fish from the wild ocean through intensive aqua-culture that is fed by wild-fish protein. Both options in fact depend on further depleting the wild ocean, a kind of "pelagic imperialism" in which powerful states and corporations collude in the desperate search for an endless "gift of nature" in more distant and deeper waters through new technologies and forms of property.[11]

Campling and Colás make the case for eras of pelagic imperialism: the whaling industry of the eighteenth century in which Dutch whalers profited through the doctrine of *mare liberum*; the rise to prominence of the New England whaling in which the *Pequod* sailed forth in *Moby Dick*; the "new imperialism" of the late nineteenth and early twentieth centuries in which Japan expanded its pelagic reach in South East Asia; the postwar period of "national" industrial fisheries in tension with the Pax Americana, which in turn expand-ed its pelagic imperialism through a network of bases and through new instruments like the Truman proclamation of the U.S. right to "conservation zones" to manage fisheries in the high seas next to U.S. coasts, using the pseudoscientific concept of "maximum fish-eries yield" (MSY) which asserted "that fishing could be sustained at high levels into perpetuity."[12] An oceanic Gramsci would ask how these waves of pelagic imperialism accumulate in specific oceanic conjunctures, as David Vine does in his book on imperial power and dispossession in Diego Garcia.[13] Another direction would be to follow the exciting directions opened up by Jesse Rodenbiker's re-search on race, class, and gender differentiation in the labor regimes of oceanic fisheries in relation to markets for high-value fish maw in Hong Kong and New York City, to show how pelagic imperialism transforms "urban oceanic relations."[14]

After the 1982 U.N. Convention on the Law of the Sea (UNCLOS), 90 percent of the world's marine-fish populations have been en-

---

11. Campling and Colás, *Capitalism and the Sea*, 181, 185
12. Campling and Colás, 187–201.
13. Vine, *Island of Shame*.
14. Rodenbiker, "Urban Oceans."

closed in EEZs as national property while they are within these areas. Was this an ocean grab by former colonizers, through the overseas territories of Britain, France, and the United States, and the white settler colonies Australia, Canada, and New Zealand, which together control a third of the total global surface area of EEZs? Campling and Colás argue that the answer is more complex, since China has a relatively tiny EEZ in per-capita terms, and since UNCLOS emerged through a process of mid-century Third World-ist assertion.[15] They argue that we should think of EEZs as "a sovereign mechanism for extracting ground rent, where the coastal state assumes the 'class function' of modern landed property."[16] We will return to these arguments about rent and decolonization in the next two chapters.

While Gramsci probably did not have the corpus of the classical agrarian question at his disposal, his elaboration through the initial recasting of the Southern Question and subsequent exploration of waves of passive revolution help us extend his own thoughts about the sea as part of his distinctive form of conjunctural diagnosis. I'd like to turn somewhat schematically to two new categories that will have to do with oceanic questions in our time in various parts of the world, and perhaps also of the world ocean as a whole. The first is a scholarly and activist category of "extractivism," and the second, which I will only touch on, is an industry category, the blue economy. I'd like to bring insights from or about these categories back to where I began, with deep-sea mining as a new form of passive revolution.

Extractivism Reconsidered

The concept *extractivismo* emerged in the Iberophone Americas in scholarship and activism detailing the wider effects of natural-resource extraction, including "neo-extractivism" under putatively

15. Campling and Colás, *Capitalism and the Sea*, 204–5.
16. Campling and Colás, 208.

leftist regimes: Hugo Chávez in Venezuela, Luiz Inácio Lula da Silva Lula in Brazil, or Evo Morales in Bolivia. The normative hopes of the concept are in forging solidarity with Indigenous resurgence and with substantively altered forms of living, relations to nature, and world-making. Key progenitor Edouard Gudynas, in the translations we have in English, argues that "extractivism" signifies more than "extractive industries" and that it is a wider mode of appropriation of nature, a new common sense and political theology. Gudynas recounts Morales raising a flask of crude oil at a hydrocarbon project like a priest with a chalice of holy wine, dipping his fingers into the oil, and anointing his ministers' helmets with the divine blood of extraction.[17] Rather than securing the terms of order, however, Gudynas argues through the work of the Renée Zavaleta Mercado that extractivism has become a field of struggle over the surpluses from appropriation of natural resources.[18] The question from Zavaleta's Gramscian perspective is how *extractivismo* galvanizes national-popular collective will in a way that is internationalist and that sustains Indigenous movement.

One strand of academic thinking on extractivism has followed the "decolonial" and linked "ontological" turn, sometimes through a renewed romance of Indigenous knowledge.[19] Another strand extrapolates broader possibilities. Michael Watts argues that "hyper-extractivism" can refer to the quantitative increase in the extraction and consumption of biomass, fossil fuels, metal ores, and nonmetallic minerals through mining, as well as through secondary extraction from used material through recycling, all of which increased from twenty-seven billion tons in 1970 to ninety-two billion tons in 2017.[20] This quantitative expansion, he argues, is part of a planetary recomposition of what Sandro Mezzadra and Brett

17. Gudynas, *Extractivisms*, 60.
18. Gudynas, 88.
19. Shutzer, Review of *Extractive Zone* by Macarena Gómez-Barris, 741–42; Chagnon et al., "From Extractivism to Global Extractivism," 13–14.
20. Watts, "Hyper-Extractivism," 209.

Neilson call "operations of capital" linking extraction, logistics, and finance in new ways. The clearest invocation of the planetary in this line of thought comes from Mazen Labban's argument that capitalist industry always involves the extraction of resource energies and of surplus value; through a consideration of biomining and recycling, he argues that contemporary extraction in both these senses takes new spatial form that is at once planetary and molecular.[21] Martín Arboleda has written a book on the topic, although it does not, to my reading, productively extend Labban's insight. Part of the problem is that Arboleda's book appears to see the planetary as a "scale" on the model of Russian dolls, a big thing out there. In contrast, Labban brilliantly poses "the planet as a living body with material capacities" everywhere, and the problem of the "becoming-mine of the planet" as "a process without beginning or end in time and space, always in the middle, *au mileu*."[22]

In a different vein, Véronica Gago and Sandro Mezzadra's "expanded concept of extractivism" includes digital mining as well as the predations of finance capital, and they argue that this exceeds the notion of exploitation through the wage relation.[23] Continuing this line of thought, Mezzadra and Neilson extend their argument about the operations of capital to the metaphorical mining of cryptocurrencies, as well as to gaming, platform urbanism, logistics, and so on, which, in their worlds, "involve heterogeneous forms of labour and exploitation."[24] I will come back to these point through Marx's "trinity formula" in the next chapter, because how we conceptualize a retreat from what is taken to be a classical Marxist notion of exploitation is important. In a final strand, Watts identifies the political economy of extraction as a regime of rent extraction, and he surmises, through reflection on Alexander Arroyo's doctoral dissertation on tech and finance from San Francisco's Bay Area

21. Labban, "Deterritorializing Extraction," 561, 572.
22. Labban, "Mine/ Machine," 151.
23. Gago and Mezzadra, "Critique of Extractive Operations," 589.
24. Mezzadra and Neilson, "On the Multiple Frontiers," 193–97.

invested in the "digital Arctic," that "extraction is less an old-world nineteenth century industry rooted in classical imperialism than a leading edge of contemporary capitalism ceaselessly searching for new frontiers of real and formal subsumption of nature."[25]

But of course, it can be both, one building on the other, depending on where and how one looks. That is what the neologism "racial capitalism" is a reminder of, the transformation of older forms of ethnoracial or imperial authority in new capitalist forms, with no presumption that any particular racial-capitalist form lasts forever. Watts's many decades of research in Nigeria's oil landscape seems to show a very complex and changing geography of rent extraction that, in the case of oil theft, relies on a mosaic of "quasi-sovereignty . . . populated by its own petty sovereigns."[26] And this is what one might expect in the complex aftermaths of imperialism across the African continent. Consider two studies of extraction that productively build on agrarian studies and show the protracted, though by no means eternal, importance of imperial forms in contemporary landscapes of capitalist extraction.

The first is the work of historian Matthew Shutzer, who looks closely at India's fossil-fuel capitalism over a century, from the 1870s to the 1970s, and particularly at the coalfields of eastern India, which have also been the site of sustained Indigenous resurgence.[27] There is a lot to commend this study, but I want to focus on the curious story of property in subterranean resources that Shutzer offers by taking seriously the idea that ground rent, in his words, "represents the sedimentation of historical struggles over who is permitted to monopolize finite reserves of land and nature," which prompts a question for him: "How do preexisting forms of landed property and ground rent come to interact with new social and ecological pressures generated by the land-intensive logic of extractive industries?"[28]

25. Watts, "Hyper-Extractivism," 213, 215.
26. Watts, 230.
27. Shutzer, "Extractive Ecologies."
28. Shutzer, "Subterranean Properties," 403.

Shutzer's response from the history of mining in colonial Bihar and Bengal is that the colonial Permanent Settlement of Bengal built on the ambiguities of *zamindari* large-landowning agrarian property, which was particularly ambiguous about the legal status of subterranean wealth; while mining companies reinforced *zamindari* in order to extract coal as tenants, this only heightened struggles over subterranean property. The attempt at fixing rights through new forms of calculation did not solve matters either, because, as Shutzer puts it concisely, "extraction does not take place in the frictionless space of scientific circulation, but much closer down to earth."[29] Perhaps this is what Gramsci means by an "earthly" form of thought that is not just a critique of speculative thought but also is attentive to ways of apprehending earthly processes. What postcolonial India inherited was the enduring "unresolved contradiction between an agrarian topsoil vested in cultivators, and a mineral subsoil vested in *zamindars* and coal companies"; and when the postcolonial state, in its wisdom, abolished *zamindari,* it effectively became "a coal *zamindar.*"[30] Property regimes over new forms of subterranean "land," Shutzer shows, have to be seen through grounded struggles over capital accumulation, custom and law.

The second study is from Gavin Capps, his 2010 doctoral dissertation, "Tribal-Landed Property," on the political economy of mining under the BaFokeng chieftaincy in South Africa from the nineteenth century to the advent of democracy in 1994. Capps takes on recent orthodoxy in African studies that has presumed that the colonial investment in chieftaincy across the continent has limited the emergence of capitalism and the usefulness of Marxist critique. I will come back to this aspect of Capps's work in the next chapter, but what he shows expertly is that chieftaincy was a colonial instrument both of domination and of capital accumulation, and that the proliferation of land deals with foreign cap-

29. Shutzer, 415.
30. Shutzer, 429–30.

ital across the African continent today are intertwined with the persistence of chieftaincy, or petty sovereignty more generally.[31]

In the late nineteenth and early twentieth centuries, the area of Bafokeng and Rustenberg, about 130 kilometers northwest of Johannesburg, saw a spate of land purchase by Africans, registered "in-trust" to the state under a recognized chief of the BaFokeng tribe; landholdings were bifurcated as either tribal-trust land with attached mineral rights or farms under a form of state land. In the 1960s, mining in this region accelerated through the auspices of Impala Platinum, which negotiated access to mining areas through the apartheid state. This racial-capitalist state of the 1970s started to offer "independence" in quotation marks to homelands, and BaFokeng was absorbed into the homeland of Bopthatswana, with its own president. When the BaFoking chieftaincy began to be more assertive in its relations with Impala, the courts empowered that the homeland president as state trustee, and he renewed Impala's lease with low royalties. Conflicts continued in democratic times, with the minister of land affairs now the state trustee, and a new minerals bill in 2002 shifted "custodianship" of minerals to the state and launched a process of racial transformation of corporate ownership, including in the mines, called Black Economic Empowerment (BEE.) The Bafokeng chieftaincy deftly shifted strategy to seek an equity stake with Impala, which satisfied Impala's BEE requirement while ridding the chieftaincy of state interference. In effect, Capps argues that tribal authority had become a form of capital.[32] What is so exciting about the work of Shutzer and Capps is that these studies add a new twist to debates about "racial capitalism" in the Black Marxist tradition by showing how ethnoracial forms can become hegemonic, leaving the overt traces of their "traditionalism" behind. To my mind, this is exactly the kind of critical diagnosis that Gramsci was engaged in.

31. Capps, "Custom and exploitation."
32. Capps, "Tribal-Landed Property," 470–74.

Terraqueous Extractivism and the "Blue Economy"

Does this matter for terraqueous extraction from the seabed, which is unlikely anywhere to be anything like the situations I have just described, in which traditional authorities might be able to claim deep-sea resources? While coastal communities have in some instances been able to fight along on the lines of landed extractive contracts, there is no such possibility on the high seas.[33] My point is broader: the extractivism of state and capital in the name of the nation is shaped by colonial histories that configure postcolonial realities, one way or the other, and even the notion of extraction through the tech-mediated digital ocean is not free of the imperial past.[34] Depending on one's theoretical and political perspective, the point is to diagnose how every instance of capital is shaped by the imperial or racial past. That is what the Black Marxist concept "racial capitalism" is a reminder of, and as both Gilmore and Keeyanga-Yamahtta Taylor argue, this is what we should simply assume of "capitalism."

I have not attended to the complexity of the notion of the blue economy, but I would point to the work of Rosanna Carver, who has been investigating its complexities as a discourse emerging from Small Island Developing States (SIDS) and from the Third World-ism of UNCLOS, but with more complex politics surrounding "resource sovereignty," particularly complex in unlocking its potential for Namibia's blue economy, in which especially phosphate mining at the point where the Benguela current wells up running along the southwest of the subcontinent will be in the national interest.[35] Carver argues that the EEZ is in fact an ambiguous vertical space of territorialization, with a surface where other states have "right

33. Many thanks to Philippe LeBillon, drawing on his long-term insights on "ocean defenders."

34. See Helmreich, "Blue-green Capital," although I cannot do it justice here.

35. Carver, "Resource Sovereignty and Accumulation."

of innocent passage" under UNCLOS, with a water column under the jurisdiction of the coastal state, and with a seabed and subsoil over which the state has sovereign rights rather than full territorial sovereignty. The terraqueous process of dredging the seabed and extracting phosphate through the water column is a complex problem that is bound to be contentious.[36] The water column brings phosphate mining into contradiction with fishing capital, further demonstrating how distant actual environmental concerns are for the wild ocean that lurks somewhere beyond the fetish of the blue economy.

I have suggested that approaches to extractive industry from agrarian studies are particularly suited to extending the insights of an oceanic Gramsci. This has taken us at various moments to questions of imperial power that Gramsci saw as central to his conception of capitalism. We turn next to think more carefully about waves of imperial power that prefigure the making of the ocean as a blue economy waiting for the predations of corporate capital.

36. Carver, 384–85.

3. Just One Last Watery Ghost-Dance?

I BEGAN THIS EXPLORATION with a reading of Gramsci on the sea and suggested that Gramsci's elaboration is tidalectical in its attention to how struggles and their intertwined concept-work accumulate, erasing and conserving elements on new shores. I then turned to the oceanic question as a heuristic like the Southern Question or the agrarian question, with pelagic imperialism and deep-sea mining in mind. I tried to show that an expanded sense of extractivism is more powerful if we work it back through terraqueous formations, with both the agrarian and Black Marxists traditions proposing, although differently, the insight that prior forms are often conserved in the new. While oceanic extraction might seem entirely a product of our time, it sublates prior imperial forms in different ways. From the perspective of our oceanic Gramsci, what appears to be an outside or a zone of difference is always already folded into the differentiated operations of hegemony through this process of sublation that neither preserves nor destroys difference completely. This chapter explores what exactly it means to attend to accumulations of oceanic imperialism without lapsing into a terracentric form of thought.

Let us consider again the ambiguous terraqueous territorialities off a coast with rich mineral deposits such as Namibia and Roasnna Carver's exposition with which the last chapter ends. Ships transit on the surface of an exclusive economic zone (EEZ), stopping at ports where they pay wharfage. Larger ports aspire to becoming quasi-autonomous entrepreneurial "landlord ports," like the Port of Oakland, not far from where I write. Fishermen of different types, scales of operation, types of boats, and fishing technology hope to continue to reap from the shifting fisheries through the water column, those with the latest technologies accruing "differential rent." Mining corporations vie for concessions to dredge the sea floor, realizing that mining phosphate nodules through the water column requires transitioning through an environment with multiple territorialities and claimants. Rents of different kinds might seem a kind of bonanza, a gift of nature from specific seabed and currents. The idea of the "blue economy" makes a virtue of such a perspective, promising to spread these gifts a bit more widely than expected while conserving their natural basis. But what remains hidden in plain sight?

"Jorge Luis Borges once remarked that the absence of camels in the Koran reveals the book's authenticity. It has its roots in a culture in which camels are taken for granted." This is Fernando Coronil's wonderful opening to his critique of the neglect of nature in Western social theory, and particularly in Marx's critique of capitalism, and Western Marxism in its wake.[1] Coronil argues that the evasion of nature and of imperialism are interconnected. He turns to Marx's "trinity formula" in the third volume of *Capital,* which tries to destabilize the formula "capital–profit, land–ground-rent, labor–wages." Rather than a trinity of equals or an axiom of causation, Marx says these three pairs "belong to widely dissimilar spheres and are not at all analogous with each other. They have about the same relation to each other as lawyer's fees, red beets and music." Capital is a historically specific social relation, not a generic factor of production, just as land is "inorganic nature . . . in all its primeval wildness" and labor is no "third party in this union[,] a mere ghost." Rather, Marx argues in the same passage:

1. Fernando Coronil, *Magical State,* 21.

> In this economic trinity represented as the connection between the
> component parts of value and wealth in general and its sources, we
> have the complete mystification of the capitalist mode of production,
> the conversion of social relations into things, the direct coalescence
> of the material production relations with their historical and social
> determination. It is an enchanted, perverted, topsy-turvy world, in
> which *Monsieur le Capital* and *Madame la Terre* do their ghost-walking
> as social characters and at the same time directly as mere things.[2]

There are several moments in Marx's oeuvre when we see ghosts
and specters, walking, dancing, and of course haunting, either as
signs of inauthenticity or as portents of things to come. Jacques
Derrida argues that all Marx hopes for is a good exorcism of the
spectral through critical analysis.[3] Capps, whose work I raise in the
previous chapter, argues that Marx intends phenomenal forms not
as false, but just not as essential. But even what Marx poses as essential to capitalism are historical and contradictory essences; they
reach fruition in their dissolution, not just in system crises, but in
ongoing struggle. This is part of Marx's intentional dramaturgy as he
lays out a contradictory, crisis-prone machine built for breakdown,
one that requires ongoing violence to quell any notion that it is not
natural and self-sustaining. Since the passages later compiled as
volume 3 of *Capital* were written before the publication of volume
1, they have implications for how we read Marx's method afresh.

Volume 1 of *Capital* famously opens out from the commodity,
its internal value form, the circulation of commodities and money,
labor-power as the source of surplus value, the transformation of the
labor process, technological change, class struggles over the working day, and the accumulation of capital and ends with a sketch of
histories of dispossession and colonization. All of this is in keeping
with his critique of the trinity formula precisely if we do not assume
that Marx intended to center the capital–labor relation, or assume

2. Marx, *Capital Volume III*, ch. 48, sec.1. "Ghost-walking" here can
also be translated "ghost-dance."

3. Derrida, *Specters of Marx*, 57–58.

that it takes an ideal form in the triad of the English working class, tenant farmer, and improving landlord. Without an English ideal type, one cannot argue that capitalism arose *there* in ideal form and then spread elsewhere. And yet this diffusionist reading of Marx as a thinker of the capital–labor contradiction ramifying across time and space is a powerful if mistaken view in some strands of metropolitan Marxism.

Agrarian Marxists attend to these matters by seeing the "English road" and its long-term, state-backed transfer of property to land-lords who rented land out to capitalist tenant farmers, who then hired the dispossessed as landless workers, as just one of several formations. Agrarians attended to multiple, differentiated geographies of change, most famously in essays by Robert Brenner and Terrence J. Byres. But what happens to the question of land in Marx's thought? That is one of Coronil's questions. Does the idea of monopoly over land and nature slip into the background? What do we make of the unholy dance of *Monsieur le Capital* and *Madame la Terre*? And why is it *monsieur' le capital* and *madame' la terre*?

In volume 3 of *Capital,* Marx writes: "Capital may be fixed in land, incorporated in it either in a transitory manner, as through improvements of a chemical nature, fertilization, etc., or more permanently, as in drainage canals, irrigation works, leveling, farm buildings, etc. Elsewhere I have called the capital thus applied to land *la terre-capital*. It belongs to the category of fixed capital."[4] Just as capital seeks to subsume historically and geographically specific forms of labor (and remember from the last chapter that attentiveness to multiple labor regimes was a key contribution of Marxist agrarian studies), capital also seeks to bring earthly and oceanic formations into circuits of capital. But some kinds of land or nature can be obstacles to capital—the Arctic ice melts, the Himalayan snow line rises, waters rise, river deltas change shape, shorelines erode—and while capital finds new avenues to produce terraqueous forms,

4. Marx, *Capital Volume III,* ch. 37.

there are increasing limits to the capacities of "geoengineering" to contain the catastrophes of our age. So, let us return to the ghost-dance, one last time.

Yutuka Nagahara writes of "the ghost-dance performed by *Monsieur le Capital* with *La Terre*/this earth . . . which is coerced to collude with *Monseiur le Capital* in the form of *Madame la Terre*; [that] . . . the secret of this dance lies in the coercively collusive relationship between landed property and capital through fixed capital, which revolves around fictitious capital."[5] There is a lot embedded in this statement, but what is key is that capital *attempts* to treat earthly formations as if they might be capitalized, and thereby controlled, with debt and finance helping enable circuits of capital for an unknown future reward. Finance capital at its heart is agnostic about what real productive activity it is meant to stimulate; it claims complete disinterest in these merely earthly hopes or fears, as the true spirit of capital. Rather than exorcising this ghastly specter, we stay with its fantasy dance.

Both Coronil and Nagahara read critically the hetero-gendering of the dance itself. As Coronil puts it, Marx's "account of the productive engagement of *Monsieur le Capital* with *Madame la Terre* unwittingly serves to confirm dominant representations of a world polarized into a masculine and creative order which is the home of capital in the metropolitan centers and a feminized and subjected domain where nature passively awaits capital's fertile embrace in the periphery."[6] This sexual grammar helps enable a progressivist reading of Marx's method in which capital's history is propelled by the capital–labor relation, which is then fixed in specific geographies, as long as the "spatial fix," as David Harvey calls it, works. But this "work" is precisely occluded by the unholy family romance, with "inorganic nature . . . in all its primeval wildness," as Marx puts it, pacified as *la terre capital*.

5. Yutuka Nagahara, "*Monsieur le Capital* and *Madame la Terre*," 947.
6. Coronil, *Magical State*, 57.

With this in mind, Coronil tries to hold Marx to his critique of the trinity formula. He draws on Henri Lefebvre to ask how the production of space and nature is occluded by the formula "capital–profit, land–rent, labor–wages." Coronil takes seriously Lefebvre's insight that the this occlusion of nature, and of earthliness in Gramsci's terms, is only going to become more significant. There is a different resonance to this formulation in our time of planetary climate emergency, with differentiated implications.

Another aspect of Coronil's critique that also draws from Lefebvre is his critique of what he calls "Occidentalist modalities" in narration about "the West and the rest," Self and Other, particularly in three modes: one in which the Other is obliterated, the second in which it is folded into the Self, and the third in which it is used to destabilize the Self. Coronil leaves the reader with how we might think beyond the reliance on West–rest or Self–Other binary relations central to all these forms of Occidentalist reason.[7] Coronil's critique is useful for its structure of thought if we consider analogously what it might mean to think beyond terracentrism, or go below the waterline, by marking when the ocean is obliterated, when it is folded into terracentrism, and when it is used to destabilize terracentrism, in each case reinstating the land–sea binary.

How might we attend to terraqueous territorialities and structures of feeling without lapsing into a background terracentrism, a land–sea binarism not unlike West–rest or Self–Other binary distinctions? This issue cannot be resolved simply by attending to matters below the waterline, to volume, wetness, acidity, or flux, even though the oceanographic aspects ought to be part of what Gramsci refers to as "organicity," or as his earthly commitment to dialectics. If Coronil looks for a route beyond Occidentalism in a mode of relation different from binary opposition, might we also look in similar ways at past and present imperialism in terraqueous relation? What might such a "post-terracentric" tidalectics look like,

7. Coronil, "Beyond Occidentalism."

if all we are left with are actual historical conjunctures of capital with singular earthly, fleshy specificities of space/nature and labor, with the state and its henchmen as redistributors of rents to keep the illusion of transparency going, to keep the ghost-dance of capital from sinking into the sea?[8]

Beyond Occidentalism: Waves of Imperialism, Oceanic Conjunctures

How do we think about imperial formations in terraqueous dialectical relation? I have suggested that Gramsci's shifting writings on passive revolution have a sense of waves of revolution and hegemony that both cancel and preserve, or sublate (*superare*), specific struggles and forms of discipline. Each conjuncture draws on the remains of prior forms, and no hegemonic form lasts forever. While Gramsci uses the term in relation to European revolutionary waves that made a world of nation states, we might keep his notes on the sea in mind as we ask how imperial power accumulates in waves that continue to shape oceanic conjunctures of the past and present. Even though the deep ocean might seem as if it were a tabula rasa, ready for corporate plunder, we might find multiple waves of imperial power have already shaped this way of seeing.

Consider Campling and Colás's periodization of three eras of oceanic capitalism: commercial capitalism (1651–1849), industrial capitalism (1850–1973) and neoliberal capitalism (1974–present.)[9] Obviously, one era doesn't end in 1849 with another beginning on New Year's Day of 1850. Gramsci's conjunctural approach refuses to separate space and time, exploring instead how imperial power accumulates through particular relations of dispossession and settlement, repression and incitement to struggle. In fact, while his categories changed across his work, he was quite steadfastly interested in exactly this task.

8. Coronil, 61. See also Capps, "Custom and Exploitation," 974.
9. Campling and Colás, *Capitalism and the Sea*, 10–11.

Consider again the debate between Hugo Grotius in his 1609 *Mare liberum* (Free sea) and John Selden's 1618 *Mare claus um* (Closed sea). This was a product of a particular oceanic conjuncture in which Grotius was conscripted to defend the Dutch East India Company (Dutch: Verenigde Oostindische Compagnie, or VOC) in their seizure of the prized Portuguese carrack the *Santa Catarina,* the sale of which increased the capital of the VOC by 50 percent; this action during wartime required the legal-ideological rebuttal of the Papal division of the non-Catholic world into Spanish and Portuguese zones, and the oceans into a Spanish *mare clausum,* from the Mar del Sur (the Pacific) to the Caribbean Sea up to the line of Tordesillas, and a Portuguese *mare clausum* comprising the Mar da Etiopía (South Atlantic) and Mar da Índia. Grotius argued that the ocean cannot and should not be appropriated by any nation, and that it should be a free zone of transit and transaction; but this was a defense of Dutch imperial right to the oceans in the name of freedom. Grotius's position helped establish territorial sovereignty as key to the military and juridical power enforcing freedom of trade and navigation. Selden's *Mare clausum* was an argument for exclusion of Dutch fishermen off Britain's coasts, and it was also an argument for territorialization of oceanic zones as fishing grounds.[10] Grotius and Selden were not two sides of an abstract debate. Their arguments emerged through the maritime geopolitics of seventeenth century mercantile empires from the East Indies to the North Sea. The arguments actually spanned Grotius life and multiple oceanic conjunctures.

Alison Rieser recasts this account in a surprising way through the argument that the biological properties and habits of the Atlantic herring helped shape the doctrine of the freedom of the seas. These tiny fish historically migrate from spawning grounds off the coasts of Britain and Scandinavia to winter in the deep Northeast Atlantic. They inhabit the surface at night and descend to the depths in day-

10. Campling and Colás, 73–74.

time as an evolutionary response to predators. A valuable source of livelihood as well as of revenue to English and Scottish landlords, merchants, and monasteries, the Atlantic herring was the topic of naturalistic observation around the North Atlantic. Timely arrivals of herring shoals were noted; nonarrivals were interpreted as divine punishment. Herring dies when removed from the sea, and it spoils quickly, and so is either eaten or preserved for transport to market. Grotius was interested in these natural properties; he thought migratory shoals reflected God's voice through the rhythms of nature. Of course, he was not thinking about herring when he wrote *Mare liberum* in relation to the lucrative East Indies. Yet, Scottish fishermen apparently heard the argument as if it had to do with the defense of their fishing grounds from Dutch fishing vessels. When James I broke with his predecessor Elizabeth's free-seas policy and sponsored a response to Grotius, ostensibly with his Scottish subjects in mind, his son Charles backed Selden's *Mare Clausaum,* and Selden's view of the sea was not the sea beyond the horizon that concerned Grotius, but rather the taxable coastal waters. Grotius, late in his life, imprisoned and then in exile, altered his position to one that permitted sovereignty in the interests of stewardship of fishing grounds and could not be convinced by Dutch merchants to rebut Selden. So, in a way, Rieser can argue that the herring had intervened in the course of the debates, even though their own populations would rise and fall as a consequence. In terms of Coronil's three post-Occidentalist modalities (erasing the Other, folding it into the Self, and using the Other to destabilize the Self), this account of the entry of the herring into the law of the sea exemplifies the second, a folding in of the oceanic into terracentric history.

A different way of thinking about oceanic conjunctures comes into view in Peter Linebaugh and Marcus Rediker's classic *The Many-Headed Hydra,* which, among other things is a study of the making of the British maritime imperial state over the long eighteenth century as a project of "hydrarchy" built through the maritime infrastructure of empire and the violent suppression of waves of struggle across all shores of the Atlantic. Part of their task is a revisionist historiography of "the Age of Revolution" to demonstrate its omnipresent violence, but also the revolutionary solidarities it did and might have produced. As C. L. R. James had insisted about preconditions for revolution in Saint Domingue, their book argues that revolutionary activity threatened the sinews of imperial capital, the maritime infrastructure itself, so that the Atlantic conjuncture was also a powerful expression of hegemony. There is a red thread running through the book, a notion of the sublation of struggle signaled by the anachronistic use of a radical keyword from our time, "multitude." chapter 4 returns to the archival challenge that the book foregrounds by turning to the work of Julius Scott and others.

When the British fiscal-military state came to power over the long eighteenth century, through its reliance on privateers and its ruthless attacks on piracy, it did so on an imperial oceanic stage in which multiple imperial powers competed over the sinews of mercantile and naval supremacy. The consequence across oceans, Lauren Benton shows us, with the Ottoman and Mughal empires in mind, was a differentiated "interimperial sea space that could not be owned but could be dominated."[11]

Sujith Sivasundaram shifts the problematic of the age of revolutions to the Indian and Pacific Oceans, in his view forgotten in the focus on the Atlantic and Caribbean. From these other shores of the global South, the age of revolution was one of British imperial counterrevolution, of "the spread of British trade and rhetorical commitments to humanity and civilization; and the spread of war, weapons and violent contests." When British colonialism arrived as a maritime event in South Africa's Cape of Good Hope in 1795 and in Île de France (Mauritius) in 1810, its ideological focus was in upholding "free trade" and policing "Jacobinism," a label bandied about in all directions including against the Dutch VOC. Sivasundaram's argument is that "the British neutralized this age of revolutions, an age of indigenous assertion, and co-opted concepts

11. Lauren Benton, cited in Campling and Colás, 78.

of liberty, free trade, reason, progress, printed expression and even projections of selfhood."[12] This is precisely the kind of differentiated event legible through Gramsci's passive revolution heuristic.

Consider Joseph Fradera's account of the destruction and reconstruction of monarchical empires through the Atlantic revolutionary cycle, as Britain, France, Spain, and United States became liberal "imperial nations." Fradera's *Imperial Nation* is a work of grand synthesis that asks how new imperial constitutions, across empires facing widespread hegemonic crises, defended the rights of metropolitan citizens in relation to noncitizens in imperial peripheries. Fradera does not attend to the intellectual lives or interventions by these denizens, unlike for instance James or many others in his wake, but Fradera does help us think about how European imperial states simultaneously preserved and modified republican ideals in the extension of imperial national territory. And yet the ocean remains a backdrop to imperial power, a constitutive absence, like Borges's camels in the Koran.

So, how might the ocean enter the narrative? Richard Drayton argues that it is only very recently, and briefly, that nineteenth-century industrial technology has been able to harness fossil fuels to create a kind of unimpeded mastery over natural energies.[13] He seems to suggest that this illusion of mastery has come and gone, and that deeper oceanographic histories might yet have lessons for us in a time of waning mastery. This is precisely the temporal structure suggested by Aravamudan in the opening passage in this book. Consider this passage from Drayton:

> Three million years ago, a fragile island of crust we call today Panama and Costa Rica, rose to connect Nicaragua to Colombia. The bridging of the Americas, and the enclosure of the Caribbean basin, caused a massive change in the world's climate. By separating the Atlantic from its sister, it prevented the dilution of all the super salty and warm water accumulated in the smaller ocean during the sum-

12. Sivasundaram, *Waves Across the South*, 2, 26, 112, 114.
13. Drayton, "Maritime Networks," 74.

mer months. North through the gap between Cuba and the Yucat-
an, mixed with some silty gifts of the Mississippi, a warm salty flow
bends around Florida, to become the Gulf Stream which later cools
and sinks deep in the North Atlantic to push a southwards stream
bending in another gyre around the south Atlantic, until the Arctic
flows into the Antarctic, scooping through another gyre to drive
eastwards into the Indian, the Pacific, with arms forcing around and
north until around the Cape, the Agulhas bends into the Benguela
current to push across to Brazil and the Caribbean, so completing
what oceanographers called "the global conveyor belt."

And he goes on: "These flows of energy establish where and how
human history is most likely to be made. They may be resisted,
. . . but they encourage particular paths of movement, particular
moments of engagement, accretion, confrontation." The Northeast
Atlantic trade winds teach us "why the Caribbean and Brazil were
the critical initial zones of European colonial adventure in the New
World. . . . Follow the south equatorial current in the Pacific and
you travel with the silver of Peru on the Manila galleon. Follow it
to the Indian Ocean and see where it slides close to the Equatorial
counter current and you understand why Mauritius was described
as the *clef des Indes* [key to India]." And many more of like descrip-
tions could be added.

There are important insights in the environmental determinism,
not just for the Age of Sail. Since almost 70 percent of the Caribbean's
waters come from the south, escaping slaves and convicts tried to
catch the Guiana current; and earlier still, Amerindian migrations
to the Antilles were from the Guianas and eastern Venezuela, as
were forms of oceanic way-finding. While, Drayton suggests that
we expect Indigenous knowledge to be the basis of anthropological,
navigational, and botanical knowledge, Simon Schaffer's work on
Newton's *Principia* (book 3) shows that the history of physics also
relied on field observation and measurement through the French
Academy of Sciences and its imperial intellectual circuit through
Senegal, Martinique, and French Guiana.[14] With Schaffer's interven-

14. Drayton, 74–75.

tion, we have a destabilizing of a terracentric and Eurocentric history of physics by subaltern and oceanic processes, akin to Coronil's third Occidentalist modality.

A more decisive destabilization of Eurocentric *thallasology* is apparent in Alexis Wick's beautifully written *The Red Sea: In Search of Lost Space,* which contrasts the centrality of the maritime in European modernity with the terrestrial geographical imagination of the Ottoman Empire. Wick's exploration is in part a geohistory of the Ottoman Red Sea, as well as an account of its historiographic absence until the sea was enframed as a scientific object. But ultimately this account of a spectral Red Sea that was and was not is meant very precisely to destabilize the combination of the European human sciences and the new imperialism that, in combination, created their geographical objects; that is the main argument, indebted to Edward Said and Timothy Mitchell. As lucid as it is, it is an account meant to destabilize the thallasology of the West.[15]

I contrast these attempts at thinking beyond terracentrism with Linebaugh and Rediker's *Many-Headed Hydra,* which opens with a ruse of natural history in a reading of Rachel Carson *as if* planetary currents set the stage for the "Herculean" task of making the violent transatlantic order. And it is a ruse because the myth of Hercules and the Hydra was part of attempts at forging hegemony over a constantly struggled oceanic space. In Rediker's work on the slave ship, the terrible animacy of the ocean comes into view in dialectical relation to the production of terror on the ship. The slave ship was a "moving reef" bringing along fish that feed on its wastes, and in particular significant numbers of sharks of different kinds, consciously encouraged to help enforce the despotic discipline of the ship as a factory for the making of slave labor. The terror of the shark was used to discipline desertion and rebellion amongst both slaves and crew. Rediker shows that human–animal relations were vitally important in a political sense. An abolitionist broadside makes this

15. Wick, *Red Sea.*

clear: "The Petition of the Sharks of Africa" satirizes the position of sharks who stand to lose their delectable floating dungeons were the slave trade to be abolished.[16]

Meg Samuelson has a wonderful response to Rediker's argument that slave ships were factories for the production of race and labor. After an engaging reading of Damien Hirst's shark tanks, Samuelson writes: "It seems, like Hirst, they [slave ships] also manufactured sharks.... Thinking with sharks compels attention to the despoila-tion of black lives and black lands by racial capitalism as well as to how this despoliation has ensnared sharks in an injurious net of cultural inscription. It brings to the fore the uneven distribution of vulnerability and grievability between and within species by surfacing the human-and-natural histories in which sharks were used to cast the majority of the human population beyond the pale of life-that-matters by reducing their status to meat."[17]

In this dialogue between Rediker and Samuelson we have a pow-erful approach to post-terracentric explanation attentive to think-ing relationally and differentially about sociocultural and natural histories, broadening questions of necropolitics to the more-than-human oceans. I have mentioned Stephanie Smallwood's *Saltwater Slavery,* which can also be read as an attempt at creating a particular "terraqueous structure of feeling" as people relived the terror of the Middle Passage as waves of slaves arrived in America's Black com-munities.[18] Another kind of post-terracentric account comes from Jennifer Gaynor's historical anthropology of the Sama maritime people, whose interdidal lives are usually written out of accounts of commercial, military, and political life that they were active partici-pants in shaping.[19] And another kind of approach is in rethinking the colonial-capitalist littorals in the marshlands on the verge of urban drainage in Debjani Bhattacharyya's study of Calcutta in *Empire*

16. Rediker, "History from below the Water Line," 292–94.
17. Samuelson, "Thinking with Sharks."
18. Thanks to Alejo Garcia Aguilera for this formulation.
19. Gaynor, *Intertidal History.*

and Ecology in the Bengal Delta. What is important in this study is
that land reclamation helps us understand in a differentiated way
the making of speculative land markets. Bhattacharya also draws
on Anuradha Mathur and Dilip da Cunha's representations of terraqueous landscapes, from the Ganga to the Mississippi.

My own research on early-twentieth-century Durban, on South
Africa's Indian Ocean coast, shows how former indentured laborers transformed neglected marshlands south of what was hoped
to be a white city, through small farming that eventually took over
the city's food system, providing cheap fruit and vegetables to the
white city and effectively creating a parallel city that was the basis
of Durban's distinctive demotic life and politics. What lies historio-
graphically forgotten, to take a page from Wick's "Red Sea," is the
Indian Ocean-ness of Durban's political life, mobilized in struggles
to end apartheid.[20]

Before leaving the topic of waves of imperial oceanics, let us
return to the sea that concerned Gramsci, and to how we might
think of the Pax Americana oceanically.

Gramsci's Sea, the Pax Americana, and the Coming Cold War

Concerning Britain's nineteenth-century rise to global industrial
and colonial dominance Britain, Campling and Colás argue that
"the Royal Navy upheld the Grotian conception of the high seas as
nobody's property, since it was only Britain that was in a position
to fully exploit the oceanic commons." This was built on the dele-
gitimization of privateering, and by the Royal Navy's privileges
of stopping and seizing maritime goods, a legacy of its antipiracy
police power. This is important for Gramsci's insight that the Pax
Americana is built on British imperial foundations. When the imperial ocean was industrialized through undersea telegraph cables,
steamship circulation of goods and people, intensified fishing and

20. Chari, *Apartheid Remains*.

whaling, and by the turn of the century, the militarization of the undersea by submarines, torpedoes, and mines, oceanic industrial capitalism was already war by other means.[21]

The naval arms race of the early twentieth century was fueled by thinkers like the American Alfred Mahan, whose 1890 book *The Influence of Sea Power upon History* argued a conception of geopolitical dominance through power over oceanic highways that effectively deprived the enemy of maritime routes. And this was ideologically key to the off-continent journey of the U.S. "Manifest Destiny" as an empire state as it moved offshore to a network of overseas naval bases. Mahan saw the importance of the Pacific Ocean to U.S. imperial power. Gramsci's concerns in Notebook 2 were precisely with this oceanic conjuncture of the interwar period and for what the Pax Americana in the Pacific would inaugurate.

I want to speculate a bit about the elements of the twentieth-century oceanic conjuncture from the perspective of transformations of oceanic hegemony. Gramsci's concepts of passive revolution and hegemony presume a field of struggle, which we attend to more carefully in the final chapter. I would like to return to Laleh Khalili's *Sinews of War and Trade* for the precision with which it centers on the unusual keyword *sinew*.[22] The *Oxford English Dictionary* defines the noun *sinew* as "a strong fibrous cord serving to connect a muscle with a bone," and also figuratively as "strength, energy, force" or "the main strength, mainstay, or chief supporting force" (as in John Ruskin's 1857 use: "The discipline of the masses has hitherto knit the sinews of battle"), and the *OED* records, since the sixteenth century, the related expression "the sinews of war, i.e. money" (as on the 1751 catastrophe of the H.M.S. Wager: "That part of the World, from whence their immense Wealth, the Sinews of War, is chiefly derived"). Finally, the verb *to sinew* is "to run through, tie together, cover over with, or with, sinews" or "to supply with

21. Campling and Colás, *Capitalism and the Sea*, 80–83

22. This section draws from Chari, "'Sinews' in *Sinews*."

sinews; to strengthen as by sinews; to nerve, harden," including in a figurative sense (as in J. Todhunger, 1878: "Sinew thy heart to hear; for death is dreadful"). *Sinew* brings together connotations of force and bounty, fibrous articulation that appears to impart its own energy and strength. The concept-metaphor emerged from intertwined histories of imperial militarism and accumulation in places "from whence wealth, the sinews of war, is chiefly derived." We might think of the verb form as the imperial imperative: sinew!

Khalili's book follows sinew-making (roads, ships, ports, railways) to show that empire's "fibrous articulations" were forged through powerful alliances that continue to benefit imperial power. The argument builds on Walter Rodney's text on imperial extraction from the African continent as reliant on infrastructure leading capital to the port.[23] Hence, the early-twentieth-century House of Saud forged an alliance with U.S. imperial power, prompting port construction and breathless transformation of the Gulf coastline portrayed in Abdulrahman Munif's *Cities of Salt*. The tax- and customs-free zone of the Emirate of Dubai made it a node of British imperial interest during the unraveling of the British Empire, part of what Vanessa Ogle calls an "archipelago capitalism" of differentiated and enclaved sovereignties meant to sinew the workings of finance capital after colonialism through havens that maintain global power and inequality today.[24]

Khalili's *Sinews* details these processes with an attention to place and circulation, drawing from work on critical logistics.[25] British capital, backed by the state, explored the transformation of Sharjah Creek and Dubai Creek; their different fates demonstrate how imperial geopolitics and the infrastructure for capital accumulation are differentially forged. Khalili's account enlivens earthly dialectics involved in dredging harbors, commodifying sand, and sinewing the Arabian Peninsula through new terraqueous territorialities of

23. Rodney, *How Europe Underdeveloped Africa.*
24. Ogle, "Archipelago Capitalism."
25. Chua, Danyluk, Cowen, and Khalili, "Introduction."

capital accumulation and political quiescence. As a consequence, maritime infrastructure appears central to the hegemonic apparatus in the peninsula at the turn of the twenty-first century and its regressive implications for decolonization and subaltern collective determination across the region. She ends with the caution that, despite Donald Trump, and now Joe Biden, courting "every two-bit tyrant and autocrat on the Arabian Peninsula," including the "the sadistic and infantile crown prince," we should take seriously the Saudi's turn towards China, whose turn to maritime sinews would certainly also interest an oceanic Gramsci.

Gramsci would also have been interested in how the Pax Americana sought its own place in a period of decolonization of some empires at a time of shoring up of U.S. and Soviet imperialism through gradations of imperial sovereignty. The United States was keen in the 1930s to distance itself from the kind of imperialism evident in Germany or Japan. As Megan Black carefully shows, the U.S. Department of Interior took the key role in this projection of U.S. interests in science and environmental management, rather than settler colonialism by other means, particularly with its Territories and Island Possessions (DTIP) in 1934, including Alaska, Hawai'i, the Virgin Islands, and Puerto Rico, followed by the "guano islands," the Philippines, Guam, and Samoa.[26] By claiming all the mineral resources on the continental shelf in 1946, the Department of Interior effectively annexed space on the scale of the Louisiana Purchase, juggling a vision of itself as defender of something called "the environment" while facilitating offshore oil and mineral extraction.[27] This was the point at which the U.N. Conferences on the Law of the Sea convened between 1956 and 1982, when the United States faced Third World lawyering around the making of an international legal regime with respect to the deep sea, beyond the continental shelf, as we see in the final chapter.

26. Black, *Global Interior*, 52.
27. Black, 148–50; see also Hamblin, *Arming Mother Nature*.

There is something important that happened with the fixing of EEZs, the territorialization of coastal waters, with implications for the accumulation of rents. Campling and Colás argue that we should think of EEZs as "a sovereign mechanism for extracting ground rent, where the coastal state assumes the 'class function' of modern landed property, because, as with private property over landed resources, access rights to fish, or exploration and extractive concessions, are 'separated from capital: it is merely the jural form and social location of ownership that has changed.'"[28] What is important about Coronil's analysis is that it shows how this conception of sovereign extraction of ground rent centralizes power in institutional and class fractions within the state in a way that is very difficult for the popular imagination to defetishize and dismantle.

Finally, the militarization of the Cold War ocean has left a powerful set of traces. The U.S. Strategic Island Concept became part of what David Vine calls a strategy of permanent war reliant on the world's largest collection of foreign military bases.[29] The sea became a nuclear zone by the end of the 1950s with the spread of the ideology of the "second-strike missile," in which nuclear missile submarines could launch a second nuclear strike after having been attacked; this diabolical logic provided the grounds for mutual deterrence. Nuclearization was also enabled by oceanic nuclear testing, after Hiroshima and Nagasaki. The United States obtained the right to govern Micronesia as a "strategic trusteeship territory" spanning close to two thousand islands and 7.8 million square kilometers. Five days after this acquisition, the U.S. Atomic Energy Commission created the Pacific Proving Grounds, and 105 atmospheric and underwater nuclear tests were performed over sixteen years. Islanders were dispossessed, certain islands were deemed depopulated, and many people and vast oceanic spaces

28. Campling and Colás, *Capitalism and the Sea,* 208, citing Capps, "Bourgeois Reform," 318.
29. Vine, *Base Nation.*

have suffered the effects of contamination. As an important book in progress by Laurel Mei-Singh shows, this has emboldened new formations of antimilitarist and anticarceral activism that draw from histories of Indigenous resistance to U.S. occupation in the Pacific.

However, we ought not to just see the toxifying of oceans as a backdrop. Adam Romero argues that toxic pesticides are not just an unfortunate byproduct of industrial agriculture; rather, California agriculture "functioned less as a market for novel pest-killing chemical products and more as a sink for the accumulating toxic wastes" of fossil-fuel industry.[30] Oceanic conjunctures like the Pacific Proving Grounds have been similar kinds of toxic sinks, as terraqueous territories and populations available for protracted suffering. As Jacob Hamblin shows, the United States, Britain, and other overdeveloped countries have dumped radioactive waste in the oceans for decades, and "in the 1950s, leading oceanographers viewed the ocean as a sewer," which was fodder for Soviet critique of its Cold War rivals, and by the 1970s and 1980s, marine scientists made a great shift from seeing the ocean floor as a sink for barrels of toxic waste to considering its threats to the future.[31] As Astrida Neimanis shows in her work on the dumping of mustard gas in the Gotland Deep of the Baltic Sea, the dumping site of between two and ten thousand tons of chemical munitions that resurface in various ways, legal regimes concerning disarmament and environmental protection cannot resolve the effects of these undersea weapons caches, leaving people and the marine environment in a state of suspension.[32]

Effectively, in all these situations, imperial states extract rents from human and nonhuman inhabitants of marine environments whose shortened lives subsidize the appropriation of their embodied ecologies as sinks for toxic waste. These are incalculable rents and subsidies. And yet, returning to Gramsci's problematic,

---

30. Romero, *Economic Poisoning*.
31. Hamblin, *Poison in the Well*, 2, 260.
32. Niemanis, "Held in Suspension," 46–49.

while the language of rent has sometimes galvanized subaltern political will, for instance in the rent boycotts in South Africa's revolutionary 1980s, it is impossible for any single category to articulate human and nonhuman collective political will across our oceanic planet. How, then, do we conceive of opposition to these processes of turning the oceans into a planetary grave?

4. The Storm

Drexciyology

Detroit electronic band Drexciya, the duo of James Stinson and Gerald Donald, were anonymous for many years, never performed live but planned to emerge in various places with little notice.[1] They performed with other groups, under aliases including the Underground Resistance, Japanese Electronics, Other Peoples Place, Doppler-effect, Akbsact Thought, and Lab Rat XL. What do we make of this Black "aquafuturism" *from* the Detroit underground but not *of* it, expressing the science fiction of American apartheid but refusing to be tied down by it. Fiercely anticommercial, refusing big labels, concerts, and tours, Drexciya was committed to making music. Stinson was for some time a long-distance trucker, and perhaps it was in traversing the length and breadth of the United States that he imagined traveling the "aquabahn," performing "aquajijutsu." Katherine McKittrick argues that "Drexciya offers anonymity as method and critique" and "a moment of relief," and that "anonymity—knowing (racial) personalities in advance and centering music and concept—briefly destabilizes the various surveillance systems that mark and make and weigh down black life," but also that "their unknowability asks what we listen,

1. Resident Advisor, "Why Drexciya Took Detroit Electro Underwater," October 16, 2018, video, 9:29, ra.co/features/3326.

or try to listen, and perhaps wonder, what unidentified identifications bring to bear on how we engage creative texts."[2]

In a rare interview, Stinson says "the basic idea is being spontaneous; . . . load up the equipment and start working; . . . there's nothing planned, no set course, the mystery of the unknown is basically what makes us tick; . . . it's like living on the edge with it."[3] He describes Drexciyan albums as "storms" emerging in different places, through work with record labels in different places that might affect different kinds of interventions. He speaks while waiting for *Harnessed the Storm* emerging with a record label in Portugal. Asked about whether the places conjured by Drexciya can exist here, he responds: "Sorry, no! This planet's gonna have to be rearranged. . . . Somebody's gonna have to hit the restart button. . . . Somebody's opened up the Pandora's Box and all hell's breaking loose, so, that's why I'm pushing the gas, I'm putting out images and things to take people away from here. . . . I'm loading up the Drexciya Arc and [have] a mind to take a trip away from here for a while."

The elsewhere to which the Drexciya Arc is headed is anywhere but "here," Detroit, and America. Gramsci was extremely interested in what he saw as the hegemonic apparatus centered on the Dearborn Ford plant near Detroit in the 1920s, a conjuncture that he named "Fordism" in relation to a differently spatialized "Americanism."[4] Stinson speaks from a very different Detroit in the ruins of Fordism. During Gramsci's decade in prison, Black migration from the South had begun to transform Detroit, but it was from the 1940s that it would do so dramatically, followed by decades of institutionalized racism, capital flight, and urban decay leading up to the late 1960s urban crisis.[5] While Gramsci could not

2. McKittrick, *Dear Science,* 53–54.

3. James Stinson, 2002 phone interview with Derek Beere, youtu.be /yPZYisZJofo.

4. See Notebook 22 in Gramsci, *Selections from the Prison Notebooks.*

5. Sugrue, *Origins of the Urban Crisis.*

have foreseen these transformations, the place of "the Negro" in his diagnosis of Americanism and Fordism remains surprising.

R. A. Judy notes that Gramsci would have been witness to the circulation of Claude McKay's report on "The Negro Question" at the Fourth Congress of the Communist International in 1922. Judy reads Gramsci's notes on the Negro question philologically, noting that, despite their thinness, Gramsci had a preliminary but historical reading of the Negro question as "symptomatic of America as a perpetual and violent pattern of globalizing, coercive transformative power" that tends "toward the consolidation of intelligence into practical political-economic thought"; the Negro fits into these dynamics as "energy converted to capital through absolute coercive force," and also as a force that might be deployed on the African continent to, "as it were, 'Negroize' Africa."[6]

Is this formulation, curious as it is, an indication that Gramsci was fundamentally anti-Black, as Frank Wilderson argues in a piece that axiomatically refuses the possibility of a Black Marxism in its first sentence, a kind of death sentence?[7] Gramsci's writes a blatantly anti-Black turn of phrase in a letter from 1931, and in a 1928 letter, he writes with alarm that "Negro music and dancing that has been imported into Europe" finds appeal "to the point of real fanaticism" through its "strong and violent impressions."[8] If our response is not just rejection, we might read Gramsci's disdain for Black music and dance as Fumi Okiji reads Theodor Adorno on jazz, not as apology, but as a relation between "jazz as critique" and what Fred Moten calls the "insight that Adorno's deafness carries."[9] We might also read Moten and Stefano Harney's "undercommons" with Gramsci's diagnosis of hegemony as a differentiated terrain of struggle; Assata

6. Judy, "Gramsci on *la questione dei negri*."

7. Wilderson, "Gramsci's Black Marx," 225. Wilderson carries this refusal through the text; it shapes what he can and cannot read. I cannot do justice to this real disagreement here.

8. Gramsci, letter to Tatiana of January 13, 1931, in *Letters from Prison, Vol II*; letter to Tatiana of February 27, 1928, in *Letters from Prison*, 128.

9. Okiji, *Jazz as Critique*, 24–25 (citing Moten *In the Break*, 179).

Shakur's changing perspective during her life underground after leaving the Black Panther Party can be read productively in this light.[10] Through this detour, we might read Drexciya as a spatial imagination of and from Detroit's undercommons, a space of Black musical invention in crisis-ridden millennial Detroit that turns from the undercommons to the undersea.

This takes us to Drexciya's founding submarine myth, in the liner notes to the 1997 album *The Quest,* which imagines pregnant African slaves thrown overboard, their babies born underwater, adapting, breathing liquid oxygen. The liner notes ask: "Are Drexciyans water breathing, aquatically mutated descendants of those unfortunate victims of human greed?" Drexciyans seem to answer Edouard Glissant's call: "Peoples who have been to the abyss do not brag of being chosen. . . . They live Relation and clear the way for it, to the extent that the oblivion of the abyss comes to them and that, consequently, their memory intensifies."[11] McKittrick puts it precisely: "The cosmogony in the liner notes of *The Quest* provide a redoubled satisfaction: a legible neo-slave narrative that promises a future. But this future, as we know, has not arrived. We are still waiting."[12] And then she listens:

> While we wait, I turn to the music itself. I read Drexciya not as necessarily emerging from a narrative of the Middle Passage *toward* an Afrofuture Aquatopia, but instead as collaborative sound-labor that draws attention to creative acts that disrupt disciplined ways of knowing. To begin, how might one describe lyricless Detroit techno. Andrew Gaerig describes the band's music as "short tracks of spackled, analog funk . . . offering occasional clues about Drexciya's sci-fi mystery . . . Wild high-pass filters . . . provide plenty of twine for James Stinson and Gerald Donald to bind their clapping 808s . . . Beautiful stylistic diversions . . . A wily slab of electro." On *Harnessed the Storm,* I hear fast tin beats atop heavy long-moving-long-shaking baselines that are animated by light green taps. On *Harnessed the*

---

10. Moten and Harney, *Undercommons*; Shakur, *Assata,* 241–43.

11. Glissant, *Poetics of Relation,* 8.

12. McKittrick, *Dear Science,* 56.

Storm I hear electronic high hats (*spa-spa-spa-spa-spa-spa*). I hear hollow echoes and deluge. On *Harnessed the Storm* I feel *bump-trap-boom* loss (trap). *Isk-isk-crash*.[13]

McKittrick comments on the primary instrument, the synthesizer, which, "as we know, can imitate different instruments: so, the moment of synthesization is about collaboration, borrowing, sharing, removing, and rewriting." What does it mean that they recorded live? McKittrick answers, "they played live into a predigital analogue recorder. What we are given, as listeners, is synthesized improvisation. They harness the storm and let it go."[14]

Shifting to a different medium of Black artistic synthesis, consider the work of Ellen Gallagher, and in particular her 2017 solo show *Accidental Records*.[15] McKittrick says of Gallagher's engagement with Drexciya: "Gallagher storms us!" Unlike other representations of Drexciyans, McKittrick notes Gallagher's are "humanoid faces embedded with the leaves of sea plants; she draws attention to underwater life (plants, shells, seaweed, scales, watery circles) that are relational to the few almost-humanoids she details in her work; . . . her undersea Drexciyans are constituted by, part of, within, fused with, and in relation to nonhuman underwater lifeforms."[16]

Gallagher is also an oceanic thinker taken by sea stories. She calls her "Watery Ecstatic" series her version of scrimshaw, the carvings

13. McKittrick, 56 (citing Andrew Gaerig, "Drexciya," and Drexciya's album *Harnessed the Storm*, youtu.be/SaU1Nh4MkSU).

14. McKittrick, 56.

15. Gallagher's exhibition can be viewed at hauserwirth.com/hauser -wirth-exhibitions/6185-ellen-gallagher-accidental-records/#films (including a video, 7:38); see also Gallagher, "Characters, Myths and Stories," interview, 2005 (originally published on PBS.org; republished by art21.org, November 2011), art21.org/read/ellen-gallagher-characters-myths -and-stories/.

16. McKittrick, *Dear Science*, 53. See also the curator Ekow Eshun on her work for the collective exhibition *"In the Black Fantastic,"* Hayward Gallery, London, 2022, video, 7:14 (discussion of Gallagher beginning at 2:45), youtu.be/a_L7tPG_pks.

seafarers made on whalebone. Tracing part of her ancestry to Cape
Verdians who migrated to Rhode Island through whaling ships,
Gallagher is intrigued by *Moby Dick*: "I think of it as an Afrofuturist
text."[17] The desire for the destructive whiteness of the whale is at
the heart of this enigmatic book. I am drawn to read her "Whale
Fall" (from the 2017 *Accidental Records* exhibition) through C. L. R.
James's reading of *Moby Dick* as an allegory of the good ship U.S.A.
on the precipice of authoritarianism. There are possible routes away
from inevitable catastrophe in *Moby Dick*. Queequeg, the South Sea
Islander, offers his bed in queer solidarity to the white-man narrator,
as well as, at the end [spoiler alert], his coffin, inscribed with the
inscrutable truths of his Indigenous people, a life raft that is also
a text that the narrator will never be able to read. And how could
he, Ishmael! Pip, the young Black cabin boy falls into the ocean and
loses his mind, and Gallagher reads it like this: "It's like he's held up
by these phantasmagoric terrors. The terror of drowning, the terror
of the below you can't see. It's this portrait of the Middle Passage.
His body has survived, but his mind has not."[18]

In "Whale Falls," other ships seem to rush in to join in the catastrophe. If the "Sea Bed" paintings from the same exhibition look
like works of natural history, closer inspection reveals faces folded
into shades of brown. Gallagher doesn't just look over the edge of
the boat. In her 2010 "Watery Ecstatic (whale fall)," she stays with
the whale carcass as it slowly descends to the ocean floor, where
it feeds a large number of organisms.[19] Philip Hoare ruminates on
this image:

17. Carolina Miranda, "Painter Ellen Gallagher's Tragic Sea Tales," *Los
Angeles Times,* November 17, 2017, latimes.com/entertainment/arts/miranda
/la-et-cam-ellen-gallagher-hauser-wirth-20171117-htmlstory.html.

18. Miranda, "Painter Ellen Gallagher's Tragic Sea Tales;" thanks to
Charne Lavery for making me think about Pip.

19. Presented in the exhibit *The Tale,* at the Gagsonian Gallery in
London, September 8–24, 2017, gagosian.com/news/museum-exhibitions
/ellen-gallagher-in-the-tale/.

The sun that raised the phytoplankton fed the zooplankton that fed the sand eels that fed the whale. The same cycle sequesters large amounts of carbon from the atmosphere, storing it for thousands of years. Men deconstructed whales for their own purposes: to yield oil, heat, and light from animals that lived in the cold dark depths. The human thirst for energy has resulted in a changed climate; the dead whale seems to repair it. There is something angelic in this fall into the darkness.[20]

But Gallagher's "angel of history" is Drexciyan. McKittrick is right—she storms us! Melody Jue writes: "The ocean flashes up in the moment of danger that is climate change."[21]

A third artist answers the call in a different way: John Akomfrah and his forty-eight-minute, three-channel video installation from 2015, *Vertigo Sea*.[22] The screens juxtapose breathtaking BBC natural-history documentary footage of the oceans, images and text that recall various social and environmental catastrophes, and staged historical reenactments that evoke nineteenth-century Romanticism. A news account demonstrating the dehumanization of African migrant crossings in the Mediterranean initially compelled Akomfrah's work that then became oceanic, part of a much larger tableau including Algerian Front de libération nationale (FLN) revolutionaries thrown into the sea, Argentinian dissidents meeting a similar fate, Vietnamese boat people, the industrial slaughter of whales, an Arctic polar bear hunt, and all of this against the backdrop of the relentless beauty of the sea and of marine life.

Historical reenactments revisit the figure looking out into the sea in contemplation, whether it is the freed Olaudah Equiano who joined an expedition to the Arctic, or Mrs. Ramsey in *To the*

20. See Philip Hoare, "I'll dream fast asleep," in *Ellen Gallagher, Accidental Records.*

21. Jue, *Wild Blue Media.*

22. John Akomfrah, *Vertigo Sea,* presented again at the Musée d'art contemporain de Montréal, February 10 through April 18, 2021, macm.org /en/exhibitions/john-akomfrah-vertigo-sea/.

Lighthouse, or the "water-gazers" looking out from the wharves of Manhattan in the opening pages of *Moby Dick.* Fragments from Herman Melville, Ralph Waldo Emerson, Virginia Woolf, and Heathcote Williams's poem "Whale Nation" offer intertitles cutting the contradictory visuals. T. J. Demos writes that the "vertigo" in the film "characterizes the effects of Akomfrah's geo-historiographic methodology, including its aesthetic function that unleashes uncanny affinities and unconscious relations between Black death and ecocide, . . . further thematized by the footage of Equiano" posing "statically in stylized tableaus, standing eighteenth-century European attire on an unidentified northern coast gazing out at sea;" in one scene he is surrounded by clocks on a beach, in what Demos calls Akomfrah's "Afro-surrealism."[23] Like Drexciya, this is Black cultural production speaking to imperiled planetarity, and none of the contemplative figures, not even Equiano, offer any consolations.

I have arrived at variations on an oceanic Benjamin alongside the promise of an oceanic Gramsci attentive to traditions of resistance to oceanic capitalism and imperialism.[24] With this chorus of Black artist-intellectuals in mind, I suggest that a Drexciyan champions the articulation of critique not by historical reconstruction—unless it is like Akomfrah's Equiano in eighteenth century garb looking out at the changing Artic ice—but by storming us. Perhaps this helps us read Gramsci's fitful experiments in historical reconstruction in his prison notes as deliberately forestalled. As we will see in the rest of this chapter, a Drexciyan Gramsci helps us conserve political hope through oceanic circuits that have provoked conceptions of "the strike," "abolition," "the international," and the refusal of planetary ecocide, all of which, in differentiated ways and combinations, conserve the possibility of storming us.

---

23. Demos, *Beyond the World's End,* 30.
24. Benjamin, see Baucom, *Spectres of the Atlantic* and *History 4°C.*

From the Strike to Abolition

To put it differently, it would be a mistake to think of "the strike," "abolition," "the international," and the anti-ecocidal as political ideologies of different times. All these imperatives are still with us. In the terms of our oceanic Gramsci, specific formations of subaltern political will come together in specific conjunctures, activated and are actualized in specific ways, and also sublated in new hegemonic formations that conserve unfinished struggles in different ways.

Consider Marcus Rediker's classic account of the emergence of the strike through new forms of sociality among seafarers of the eighteenth century: "The coexistence and integration of diverse types of labor, the coordination of efforts to combat a menacing laboring environment, the steady shifts of work as organized by the watch system, and the interdependence of the stages of production combined to produce a laboring experience uncommon to the first half of the eighteenth century. The seaman, in sum, was one of the first collective workers."[25] As a consequence of the slow and steady collective organizing, forged through the specific terraqueous territoriality of the seafarer's labor regime, British seamen decided in 1768 to "strike" their sails to bring maritime commerce in the pool of London to a halt, and in so doing they joined a motley London working class of weavers, hatters, sawyers, glass grinders, coal heavers and other artisans refusing their wages and working conditions.[26] However, this wasn't the only connotation to striking the sails: for much of the seventeenth and eighteenth centuries, Greg Grandin argues, the act signified submission to conquerors or to superior ships; Philippe LeBillon adds an important coda that the French *affaler,* with Dutch/Flemish roots, signifies ships removing or "falling" sails in submission to high winds. For seamen to revolutionize this concept from within the genealogy of seafaring praxis was more

25. Rediker, *Between the Devil and the Deep Blue Sea,* 111.
26. Rediker, 110.

precisely a refusal of submission.[27] And while "the strike" shifted and resonated in other contexts, as in the mass refusal of Indian *lascar* to labor as seafarers in 1914, described by G. Balachandran, it has become one of our most potent signs of protest.[28]

In my own research on Durban, South Africa, a dockworkers' strike in 1972 spilled out into a seemingly uncontrollable set of strikes across the city, linking university student activists with a new Black student movement that became the Black Consciousness Movement, in a complex and multifaceted urban revolt called "the Durban Moment." By one account, the dockworkers strike sparked the internal struggle that took various forms through the 1970s and 1980s and that was crucial to the end of apartheid. In one of the neighborhoods that I write about, this was paralleled by a strike wave across the churches, as predominantly women-led congregations imagined taking hold of their religious life as well. There is an archival silence about the oceanic origins of this strike wave in a port city that may have been a key element in the end of apartheid, as well as about the other kinds of strikes it engendered.[29]

The idea of multiplicity of strikes resonates with the transformations of the strike in our time: the prison strike, often linked to the hunger strike, as at various times in Ireland, Palestine, or Turkey; the feminist strike with Ni Una Menos in Argentina; the student-debt strike in the United States; the George Floyd uprisings as a strike against policing; tenant strikes in various cities; and, still, seafarers strikes and strikes along the commodity chain; airline-workers strikes; logistical strikes like the Amazon warehouse workers strikes during the pandemic.[30] Then, there is the idea of the general strike

27. Grandin, *Empire of Necessity*; Philippe LeBillon, personal communication, Janurary 17, 2023.

28. Balachandran, *Globalizing Labour*, 245.

29. Chari, *Apartheid Remains*, ch. 6.

30. Thanks to the *Critical Times* editorial team for discussions toward a special issue on "strikes," read.dukeupress.edu/critical-times/issue/5/3.

in which all kinds of workers down tools in solidarity to refuse to continue business as usual. The important point is to think about the strike not just as a disruption in the capital–labor relation, but as a disruption of the fiction of the holy "trinity formula."

The general strike takes us to the question of what comes next: is it what Ruthie Gilmore calls the restoration of capital by using capital to save capital from capital, which takes us back to Gramsci's heuristic of passive revolution. We now know from a very wide historiography that a multiplicity of labor regimes, forms of tenancy, and types of indebtedness induce a variety of forms of hegemony through the land–labor–money nexus, differentiating people and places in what we now call "racial capitalism" or the differentiated survival of capitalism, its capacity to both absorb and produce social and spatial difference.[31] But what does it mean to imagine the end of capitalism, and why is it more unimaginable than the end of the world?

Alberto Toscano argues that "following a leitmotif in Marx's own writings, echoing a broader communist discourse that exceeds and precedes him, a discourse that Marx did not create *ex-nihilo,* the major name for this undoing is indeed *abolition.*" Marx and his contemporaries used the term *aufhebung,* usually translated *sublation* in English, but Toscano notes that work from France, including from Lucien Seve and Patrick Theuret, reads *aufhebung* as overcoming or moving beyond, with an element of conservation, in contrast to the other term Marx and others use, *auslöchen,* for extinguishing the slave trade or private property. Toscano calls attention to Seve's translation of *aufhebung* as *depassement,* a moving through, before turning to police abolition today with Gilmore as an interlocutor, concluding with Jacques Camatte's notion of communism as "the resurrection of dead labor." In another piece that continues this line of thought, Toscano responds to Camette and to Moishe Postone to say that we should resist the temptation

---

31. Chari, "Interlocking Transactions."

to think of capital's production of sameness without also attending
to its production of difference.[32]

Why does all this matter: because if *abolition* as *aufhebung* names
a *depassement*, a moving through in which some things are cancelled and preserved not just in the realm of the ideological but in
embodied, material, spatial, and ideological relations, and in the
production of sociospatial differentiation, that is exactly what we
see in the history of abolition of slavery. When Akomfrah directs a
historical reenactment of Equiano after emerging from horrors of
the slave trade through abolitionism, looking out at the devastation
of the marine world, he literally stages a scene of *depassement* that
pushes us to think beyond to ask what in fact has been abolished
and what has not.

This line of thought helps us read W. E. B. Du Bois as fundamentally concerned with the cancelation/preservation of the trinity of
land–labor–money relations in the aftermath of slave-based plantation capitalism rather than with a more foundational and Black
reconstruction; that is why *Black Reconstruction in America* culmi-
nates in the rearticulation of whiteness as property.[33] Kris Manjapra
puts it concisely: "When white societies actually began *implement-
ing* their antislavery ideas, they did so in ways that prolonged and
extended the captivity and oppression of black people around the
world."[34] Several historical studies have shown us how the discourse
of abolition and emancipation was used to extend other kinds of
unfree labor, shedding different light on the insights of Marxist
agrarian studies on the persistence of differentiated labor regimes.

The other key element of emancipation was that granting repa-
rations to slave owners was a windfall to slave-owning plantation
owners who reinvested capital widely, including in slave-based
plantations in the United States, Brazil, and Cuba; in plantations

32. See Alberto Toscano, "Abolition Philosophy," video, 1:17:25, youtu
.be/NYDKHG7OmrE; Toscano, "The World is Already without us."

33. Du Bois, *Black Reconstruction in America.*

34. Manjapra, *Black Ghost of Empire,* 5.

reliant on indentured and other kinds of unfree labor in Guyana, Trinidad, Dominica, Honduras, South Africa, Sri Lanka, Malaysia, and Australia; in the shipping of indentured laborers across the global plantation belt; and in other kinds of colonial infrastructure including shipping, railways, and finance—in other words, in the sinews of nineteenth century colonial capitalism.[35] The failure of "Black reconstruction" also spurred the globalization of Jim Crow. Marilyn Lake and Henry Reynolds show how, in this process, circuits of expertise invested in limiting democracy worked across what were hoped to be "white men's countries," redrawing a global color line.[36] Carl Nightingale's history of urban segregation shows how early experiments in "city-splitting" moved out from colonial Madras and Hong Kong, across the hill stations of colonial Asia, across the Indo-Pacific, and across to South Africa with the bubonic plague as pretext, giving South African cities the opportunity to engage in coercive urban transformation. The key point is that the term *segregation* spread across languages and contexts, taking different shapes in the long backlash against abolitionism.[37]

Scholars interested in Black and subaltern intellectuals who became critics of "global Jim Crow" think in the wake of the late Julius Scott's *The Common Wind,* which explored the vast, clandestine web of communication across eighteenth-century Caribbean plantation societies and the ways in which revolutionary ideas spread across the sea of islands before and after the Haitian Revolution. Despite the efforts to limit the spread of information, slaves and other subalterns were sometimes better informed than their erstwhile masters; and this is important for any conception of abolition attentive to what remains after the counter-revolutionary offensive sets in.[38]

Methodologically, Scott pushes us to think as capaciously as possible about the archives of the dispossessed. We might read Saidiya

35. Manjapra, 107.
36. Lake and Reynolds, *Drawing the Global Colour Line.*
37. Nightingale, *Segregation.*
38. Scott, *Common Wind.*

Hartman's *Wayward Lives* as another powerful response that bridges the furtive intimate lives of Black and queer women just off the margins of the archive.[39] We might consider the powerful work of Indian Ocean radical Françoise Vergès, who was once charged with constructing a museum of indenture in her homeland of Reunion Island, which she conceptualized as a museum without objects, for people who did not leave a trace. This unimaginably brilliant idea was of course too radical to actually be implemented.

There are other ways to think of traces of the dispossessed, keeping Drexciya and Paul Gilroy's *Black Atlantic* in mind.[40] Michael Denning argues that "the audiopoetics of a world musical revolution" forged through the sinews of empire between the onset of electrical recording in 1925 and the Great Depression of the 1930s produced a world of musical communication across "barrios, bidonvilles, barrack-yards, arrabales, and favelas of an archipelago of colonial ports, linked by steamship routes, railway lines, and telegraph cables," connecting plebian music and dance cultures to an emergent anticolonialism that made possible "the decolonization of the ear and the dancing body" before anything else.[41] Denning's earthy, embodied materialism offers a way of practicing Gramsci's "earthliness of thought."

Another fascinating study is Drexciyan in a different way. Sumathi Ramaswamy's spellbinding *The Lost Land of Lemuria* traces the transformation of European scientific imaginations of the 1860s as they travelled to Tamil-speaking South India, drawing in a range of figures invested in the fabulation of Lemuria as a lost Tamil continent in the Indian Ocean. Ramaswamy diagnoses the scholarly, literary, visual, and cartographic profusion around Lemuria just as a disenchanted form of colonial geography was becoming commonplace as the ground of critique of the colonial and its aftermath. There is more to the timing of these labors of loss of a prelapsar-

39. Hartman, *Wayward Lives, Beautiful Experiments*.
40. Gilroy, *The Black Atlantic*.
41. Denning, *Noise Uprising*, 38, 137.

ian and deep-historical Tamil past at the end of empire. They come at precisely at the moment of consolidation of mid-century Tamil nationalism in the wake of the wide-ranging Self-Respect Movement, which in its most radical phase called for the abolition of Brahminism, bonded labor, and priest-mediated marriage, and for the dawn of a new age of mutual respect. The transformation of this movement is another opportunity to think with Gramsci's heuristic of passive revolution, and to consider varied entailments of the continued investment in Lemuria. Our Drexciyan Gramsci might ask in our time how various subalterns might deploy the fabulation of Lemuria to index ongoing terraqueous dispossession and destruction along the deltas and coasts of the Tamil country.

Oceanic Internationalism and the Refusal of Ecocide

Another concept with a contradictory relationship to the ocean is "the international." Samera Esmeir argues that *international* entered the English language in 1789, coined by Jeremy Bentham as a re-framing of the "law of nations," bringing into being a conception of "a distinct legal space for the regulation of inter-space relations."[42] Bentham's conception of the earth as a two-dimensional surface divided by nations through the tools of geography and cartography was quite different from Hugo Grotius's conception from his 1609 *Mare liberum* (The free sea), in which, in Esmeir's words, "the ocean was indeed a material surface to be traversed (by colonists and merchants.) But it was not only that. It shared its moisture with the skies, the clouds, and the stars. . . . It exceeded human cognition, human calculation. The earth, including its oceans, was not only a surface; it was also the seat of humankind, one planet among others."[43]

International as adjective and noun took other travels as well, for instance in the International Workingmen's Association, for which,

42. Esmeir, "On Becoming Less of the World," 88.
43. Esmeir, 95.

Esmeir argues, "the adjective *international* gained a socialist revolutionary itinerary—one with experiences and horizons of expectation distinct from its juridical itinerary."[44] Although these expectations shifted in the noun form of the First and Second Internationals, expressive of something closer to Bentham's concept, we should hold onto the possibilities of the revolutionary conception of internationalism as we turn to the oceans at the moment of the Asian African Conference at Bandung in 1995.

Turning to Bandung and the sea, Esmeir begins with Indonesian President Sukarno's recognition that the oceanic waterways of imperial power were quite literally a poisoned gift in that the "oceans and seas could transform into lifelines of other forms of human horror, domination, and destruction that would affect current and future generations," and the forms of solidarity proposed by Bandung were precisely a refusal of this inevitability.[45] But the anticolonial impulse at Bandung was limited, indeed disciplined, by its commitment to sovereignty, and to the conception of a world produced by international cooperation among decolonized sovereign states. Sukarno was responding to the transformation of the doctrine of the freedom of the seas in the twentieth century as an enabler of European colonization, but without troubling its foundational commitment to the sea, as Esmeir puts it, as "the constitutive cement for staging an enlarged world, . . . a unified world and, more significantly, spatial-political possibilities for capturing it and intervening in it."[46]

A new generation of Third World lawyering, including those associated with the movement Third World Approaches to International Law (TWAIL) focused precisely on how the changing approach to the law of the seas privileged some countries' capacities "to exploit the resource of the sea, to terrorize the world and to destroy the

44. Esmeir, 89.
45. Esmeir, "Bandung," 82.
46. Esmeir, 85.

marine environment."[47] In this view, leaving the high seas to the doctrine of freedom of the seas would only continue to privilege imperial powers. The venue for these debates was a series of U.N. conferences leading up to the 1982 U.N. Convention on the Law of the Seas (UNCLOS.)

The Third World did not always speak in unison in these debates. Surabhi Ranganathan argues that India equivocated on supporting the Latin American demand for limiting natural jurisdiction of the sea bed to two hundred miles, preferring to join a bloc of "margineers," including the United States, the United Kingdom, Australia, New Zealand, and Canada, who argued for a limit of six hundred miles. First world countries were joined by the U.S.S.R. in contesting the demand that the exploitation of the deep sea be conducted through an international body, "the Enterprise"; industrialized states argued that the deep seabed should continue to adhere to the freedom of the seas.[48]

Despite these contradictions, as a consequence of Third World lawyering, a set of principles were codified into law. Under the first principle, coastal states could declare an exclusive economic zone (EEZ) up to two hundred nautical miles (230 miles); "as long as they did not overexploit living resources"; the second principle declared "the sea bed, ocean floor and subsoil beyond the limits of national jurisdiction and consisting in an 'Area' that is the 'common heritage of mankind,'" and that the International Seabed Authority would adjudicate matters in this "Area."[49] Esmeir summarizes the consequence:

> If Grotius's doctrine constituted an enlarged surface of the world for colonial free exploitation, the new doctrine of UNCLOS introduced some limitations on *laissez-faire* in the form of exclusive economic zones and Common Heritage of Mankind (CHM). Arguably, additional advocacy is required to preserve a more expansive marine en-

---

47. Ram Prakash Anand, cited in Esmeir, "Bandung," 86.
48. Ranganathan, "Decolonization and International Law," 170–73.
49. Esmeir, "Bandung," 87–88.

vironment, including its animate and inanimate lives. Yet under UN-CLOS, the limit of this Area, no matter how expansive it will be is the surface of the sea; the commons of humankind is inside the sea. The sea is split into two: one where competing sovereigns can navigate the ocean's surfaces and project themselves onto them, and another whereto humankind can descend to preserve its heritage (while also failing to counter the destruction of the commons). Crucially, the former is the condition of possibility of the latter in the form of an outer limit; the heritage of humankind in the depths of the sea is conceivable only once its surface has been detached as a distinct but enlarged domain for sovereign states.[50]

Effectively, this legal structure has sustained sovereignty over the sea, and by extension the power of capital. As Ranganathan clarifies, the division of the seabed and the seawater includes a further complication: "The seabed up to 200 miles may be both the continental shelf and the EEZ of a state, but it is governed solely as the former. Furthermore, unlike in the case of the continental shelf, a state must expressly proclaim an EEZ. Absent such a proclamation, the waters beyond the territorial seas are treated as the high seas, although the bed remains the continental shelf."[51] While the seabed is differentiated from seawater, "'sedentary' living resources are placed within the continental shelf regime; ... they include bottom-dwelling creatures such as clams, oysters, sponges and corals, ... [as well as] crustaceans, such as shrimps, prawns, lobsters and crabs, even though these can swim"; meanwhile, fish that breed on the seabed are part of the seawater regime, whether as part of the EEZ or the high seas.[52]

Esmeir asks what was lost in Bandung, if not other ways of being with and traversing the seas, and she turns to the work of Sunil Amrith as a way of tracing formations of oceanic internationalism that do not reinforce sovereignty and capital, and that might confront the struggles necessary to prevent the further poisoning of the seas.

50. Esmeir, 89.
51. Ranganathan, "Ocean Floor Grab," 588.
52. Ranganathan, 590.

Amrith's environmental history of the Bay of Bengal connects natural history to the "people's sea." He shows how the material infrastructure of life shifts from a "maritime highway between India and China, navigable by mastery of its regularly reversing monsoon winds" to a new regime linking steamships powered by fossil fuels, plantation production fueled by indentured labor, and "imperial laws that both uprooted and immobilized people" in new ways.[53] In the aftermath of the Great Depression and World War II, during the decline of the British Empire, Amrith shows how the Bay of Bengal entered a period of fragmentation of politics, mobility, trade, livelihood, and imagination as well. The era of nation states and intensified development ushered in a new phase of despoliation and destruction of the highly populated littoral of the bay, while networks of interaction were increasingly strained, or indeed destroyed.[54]

There are hints of a Gramscian attentiveness to an earthly materialism in Amrith's attention to the effects of industrialization in the bay's hinterlands, and in the bay itself as "a frontline of Asia's experience of climate change."[55] The deep ocean and undersea tectonic plates are vital forces, for instance in the undersea earthquake of 2004 that led to the devastating tsunami across various shores. Another major oceanographic process with key sociocultural effects is, of course, the monsoon, and it changed along with coastlines and shorelines in an increasingly heated, fish-depleted, much-trashed sea by the second half of the twentieth century.[56]

The bay's fragmentation intensified in the transition to a world of nation states, leading to what Amrith calls "the final enclosure of the Bay—the treatment of the sea as an extension of national territory—[which has] facilitated its overexploitation as a resource."[57] In what

53. Amrith, *Crossing the Bay of Bengal*, 1–2.
54. Amrith, 5.
55. Amrith, 4–5.
56. Amrith, 10, 30.
57. Amrith, 260.

has become a familiar oceanic account of plastic detritus, depleted fish stocks, eroding coastlines, and destroyed mangroves, Amrith writes in defense of the "climate refugees" on the edges of the bay. With Esmeir and Gramsci in mind, we can read Amrith's argument as centered on popular determination of the terraqueous future, picking up on traces of regional sociocultural and material process-es, traces left in agrarian ecologies, built environment, and ritual practices.

For instance, Amrith notes shops along the passage to the main shrine in the Tamil town of Nagore selling images of ships to be used in prayer for voyages across the Bay of Bengal.[58] Across the bay, in Penang and Singapore, and across Burma, Ceylon, Indonesia, and Vietnam, shrines called Nagore Durgah reference their Tamil counterpart. Syncretic public cultures across the bay continue to hold traces of older debates about nationalism, reform, revolution and anticolonial struggle. In our oceanic Gramsci's terms, these are elements of the past that might yet surface to reconstitute subaltern political will in a regional and internationalist spirit, one hospitable to the stranger, to struggles for social and environmental justice, and to the nonhuman oceanic world that is inextricable from the distinctiveness of the Bay of Bengal.

Esmeir concludes that "what remains of the spirit of Bandung is the act of gathering, of the initiation of collective power and agency," and that, while this power was effectively captured by sovereignty, it also "manifested the possibility of another collectivity or being-in-common, bringing back forms of life that were once possible."[59] This is what I have also suggested is the Drexciyan capacity to "storm" our time with the imperatives of collective and planetary life.

Today we witness a new kind of race to space, and legal struggles over outer-space resources are fought on a terrain shaped by the ascendance of national sovereignty and territory at sea.[60] I have

58. Amrith, 89.
59. Esmeir, "Bandung," 93.
60. Thanks to Samera Esmeir for this insight.

not touched on the many ways in which the question of ecocide is understood today, but key debates center on using capital to save capital from capital, to paraphrase Gilmore again. Ashley Dawson has been writing against initiatives like the U.N. Convention on Biological Diversity of 2008, which promotes the marketing of environmental services and the use of offsets to foster "natural capital."[61] He reminds us that extinction is not containable. There is no way to secure islands of ecological diversity in a planetary onslaught by capitalism. The extraction of rents to benefit the few cannot save the conditions for the reproduction of capital itself.

And so, we return in the face of determinate social and natural dangers to an oceanic Gramsci attentive to waves of struggle, to the intensified surfacing of deep contradictions, to waves of passive revolution that attempt to subsume pervasive if differentiated struggles over the conditions of life. As the imprisoned Gramsci speaks to his young son Delio, reminding him to regard the teeming life of the sea, we must refuse just one last ghost-dance of *Monseiur le Capital* and *Madame la terre* in order to imagine solidarity with our most fabulous Drexciyan selves who have already learnt how to breathe liquid oxygen, living with the beautiful diversity that is somewhere just beyond the next wave.

61. Dawson, *Extinction*, 83.

Bibliography

Aravamudan, Srinivas. "The Catachronism of Climate Change." *diacritics* 41, no.3 (2013): 6–30.

Amrith, Sunil. *Crossing the Bay of Bengal: The Furies of Nature and the Fortunes of Migrants.* Cambridge, Mass.: Harvard University Press, 2013.

Baucom, Ian. *Specters of the Atlantic: Finance Capital, Slavery, and the Philosophy of History.* Durham, N.C.: Duke University Press, 2005.

Baucom, Ian. *History 4°C: Search for a Method in the Age of the Anthropocene.* Durham, N.C.: Duke University Press, 2020.

Balachandran, G. *Globalizing Labour? Indian Seafarers and World Shipping, c.1870–1945.* New Delhi: Oxford University Press.

Bhattacharya, Debjani. *Empire and Ecology in the Bengal Delta: The Making of Calcutta.* Cambridge: Cambridge University Press, 2018.

Black, Megan *The Global Interior: Mineral Frontiers and American Power.* Cambridge, Mass.: Harvard University Press, 2018.

Braudel, Fernand. *The Mediterranean and the Mediterranean World in the Age of Philip II.* 2 vols. 1973; repr. Berkeley and Los Angeles: University of California Press, 1995.

Campling, Liam, and Alejandro Colás. *Capitalism and the Sea.* London: Verso, 2021.

Carver, Rosanna. "Exploring the blue economy: Resource Sovereignty Seabed Mining in Namibia." PhD diss., Lancaster University, 2019.

Rosanna Carver, Rosanna. "Resource Sovereignty and Accumulation in the Blue Economy: The Case of Seabed Mining in Namibia." *Journal of Political Ecology* 26, no. 1 (2019): 381–402.

Capps, Gavin. "Tribal-Landed Property: The Political Economy of the BaFokeng Chieftaincy, South Africa, 1837–1994." PhD diss., London School of Economics and Political Science, 2010.

Capps, Gavin. "Custom and Exploitation: Rethinking the Origins of the Modern African Chieftaincy in the Political Economy of Colonialism." *Journal of Peasant Studies* 45, no. 5–6 (2018): 969–93.

Capps, Gavin, "A Bourgeois Reform with Social Justice? The Contradictions of the Minerals Development Bill and Black Economic Empowerment in the South African Platinum Mining Industry." *Review of African Political Economy* 39, no. 132 (2012): 315–33.

Chagnon, Christopher W., Francesco Durante, Barry Gills, et al. "From Extractivism to Global Extractivism: The Evolution of an Organizing Concept." *Journal of Peasant Studies* 49, no. 4 (2022): 760–92.

Chari, Sharad. "'Sinews' in *Sinews*," review of *Sinews of War and Trade* by Laleh Khalili. *Dialogues in Human Geography* 12, no. 12 (2020): 344–47.

Chari, Sharad. "'Interlocking Transactions': Micro-Foundations for 'Racial Capitalism.'" In *Ethnographies of Power: Working Radical Concepts with Gillian Hart,* edited by Sharad Chari, Mark Hunter, and Melanie Samson, 49–75. Johannesburg: Wits University Press, 2022.

Chari, Sharad. *Apartheid Remains*. Durham, N.C.: Duke University Press, forthcoming.

Chua, Charmaine, Martin Danyluk, Deborah Cowen, and Laleh Khalili. "Introduction: Turbulent Circulation: Building a Critical Engagement with Logistics." *Environment and Planning D: Society and Space* 36, no. 4 (2018): 617–29.

Chatterjee, Partha. *Nationalist Thought and the Colonial World: A Derivative Discourse*. 1986; repr. Minneapolis: University of Minnesota Press, 1993.

Coronil, Fernando. "Beyond Occidentalism: Towards Nonimperial Geohistorical Categories." *Cultural Anthropology* 11, no. 1 (1996): 51–87.

Coronil, Fernando. *The Magical State: Nature, Money, and Modernity in Venezuela*. Chicago: University of Chicago Press, 1997.

Corbin, Alain. *The Lure of the Sea: The Discovery of the Seaside in the Western World, 1750–1840* Berkeley: University of California Press, 1994.

DeLoughrey, Elizabeth, and Tatiana Flores. "Submerged Bodies: The Tidalectics of Representability and the Sea in Caribbean Art." *Environmental Humanities* 12, no. 1 (2020): 132–66.

Demos, T. J. *Beyond the World's End: Arts of Living at the Crossing*. Durham, N.C.: Duke University Press, 2020.

Denning, Michael. *Noise Uprising: The Audiopolitics of a World Musical Revolution*. London: Verso, 2015.

Derrida, Jacques. *Specters of Marx: The State of the Debt, the Work of Mourning and the New International*. Translated by Peggy Kamuf. New York: Routledge, 1993.

Davidson, Arnold. "Gramsci and Lenin, 1917–1922." *The Socialist Register* (1974): 125–50.

Dawson, Ashley. *Extinction: A Radical History*. New York: OR Books, 2016.

Drayton, Richard. "Maritime Networks and the Making of Knowledge." In *Empire, the Sea and Global History: Britain's Maritime World, c. 1760 – c. 1840,* edited by David Cannadine, 72–82. London: Palgrave Macmillan, 2007.

Du Bois, W. E. Burghardt. *Black Reconstruction in America, 1860–1880.* New York: Free Press, 1998.

Esmeir, Samera. "Bandung: Reflections on the Sea, the World, and Colonialism." In *Bandung, Global History, and International Law: Critical Pasts and Pending Futures,* edited by Luis Eslava, Michael Fakhri, and Vasuki Nesiah, 81–94. Cambridge: Cambridge University Press, 2017.

Esmeir, Samera. "On Becoming Less of the World." *History of the Present* 8, no. 1 (2018): 88–116.

Fanon, Frantz. *The Wretched of the Earth.* Translated by Constance Farrington. New York: Grove, 1965.

Fradera, Josep M. *The Imperial Nation: Citizens and Subjects in the British, French, Spanish and American Empires.* Princeton, N.J.: Princeton University Press, 2018.

Gago, Verónica, and Sandro Mezzadra. "A Critique of Extractive Operations of Capital: Toward an Expanded Concept of Extractivism." Translated by Liz Mason-Deese. *Rethinking Marxism* 29, no.4 (2017): 574–91.

Gallagher, Ellen. *Accidental Records.* Los Angeles: Hauser and Wirth, 2017.

Gaynor, Jennifer. *Intertidal History in Island Southeast Asia: Submerged Genealogy and the Legacy of Coastal Capture.* Ithaca, N.Y.: Cornell University Press, 2016.

Fiori, Giuseppe. *Antonio Gramsci: A Life.* Translated by Tom Nairn. 1970; repr. London: Verso, 1990.

Gilmore, Ruth Wilson. "Fatal Couplings of Power and Difference: Notes on Racism and Geography." *Professional Geographer* 54, no. 1 (2002): 15–24.

Gilroy, Paul. *The Black Atlantic: Modernity and Double Consciousness.* Cambridge, Mass.: Harvard University Press, 1993.

Gilroy, Paul. *After Empire: Melancholia or Convivial Culture?* Abingdon, Va.: Routledge, 2004.

Glissant, Édouard. *Poetics of Relation.* Translated by Betsy Wing. Ann Arbor: University of Michigan Press, 1997.

Gramsci, Antonio. *Selections from the Prison Notebooks.* Edited and translated by Quintin Hoare and Geoffrey Nowell Smith. New York: International, 1971.

Gramsci, Antonio. *Letters from Prison.* Translated by Lynne Lawner. London: Quartet, 1973.

Gramsci, Antonio. *Selections from Political Writings, 1921–1926.* Translated by Quintin Hoare. London: Lawrence and Wishart, 1978.

Gramsci, Antonio. *Prison Notebooks.* 3 vols. Translated by Joseph Buttigieg. New York: Columbia University Press, 1992–2007.

Gramsci, Antonio. *Antonio Gramsci Reader: Selected Writings, 1916–1935.* Edited by David Forgacs. New York: New York University Press, 2000.

Grandin, Greg. *Empire of Necessity: Slavery, Freedom, and Deception in the New World*. New York: Metropolitan, 2014.

Greenpeace. *In Deep Water: The Emerging Threat of Deep Sea Mining*. Amsterdam: Greenpeace International, 2019.

Gudynas, Edouardo. *Extractivisms: Politics, Economy and Ecology*. New York: Columbia University Press, 2021.

Hall, Stuart. *Hard Road to Renewal: Thatcherism and the Crisis of the Left*. 1988; repr. London: Verso, 2021.

Hall, Stuart. "David Scott." *Bomb* 90 (January 1, 2005), bombmagazine.org /articles/david-scott/.

Hart, Gillian. *Rethinking the South African Crisis: Nationalism, Populism, Hegemony*. Athens: University of Georgia Press, 2014.

Hamblin, Jacob. *Arming Mother Nature: The Birth of Catastrophic Environmentalism*. New York: Oxford University Press, 2013.

Hamblin, Jacob. *Poison in the Well: Radioactive Waste in the Oceans at the Dawn of the Nuclear Age*. New Brunswick, N.J.: Rutgers University Press, 2018.

Hartman, Saidiya. *Wayward Lives, Beautiful Experiments: Intimate Histories of Riotous Black Girls, Troublesome Women, and Queer Radicals*. New York: Norton, 2019.

Helmreich, Stefan. "Blue-green Capital, Biotechnological Circulation and an Oceanic Imaginary: A Critique of Biopolitical Economy." *BioSocieties* 2 (2007): 287–302.

Hofmeyr, Isabel. *Dockside Reading: Hydrocolonialism and the Custom House*. Durham, N.C.: Duke University Press, 2022.

Hessler, Stephanie, ed. *Tidalectics: Imagining an Oceanic Worldview through Art and Science*. Cambridge, Mass.: MIT Press, 2018.

James, Cedric Lionel Robert. *Mariners, Renegades and Castaways: The Story of Herman Melville and the World We Live In*. 1953; repr. Lebanon, N.H.: Dartmouth College Press, 1985.

Judy, R. A. "Gramsci on *la questione dei negri*: *Gli intellettuali* and the Poesis of Americanization." In *Gramsci in the World,* edited by Frederick Jameson and Roberto Dianotto, 164–78. Durham, N.C.: Duke University Press, 2020.

Jue, Melody. *Wild Blue Media: Thinking through Seawater*. Durham, N.C.: Duke University Press, 2020.

Karatani, Kojin, and Joel Wainwright. "'Critique is Impossible without Moves': Interview of Kojin Karatani by Joel Wainwright." *Dialogues in Human Geography* 2, no. 1 (2012): 30–52.

Khalili, Laleh. *Sinews of War and Trade: Shipping and Capitalism in the Arabian Peninsula*. London: Verso, 2020.

Khanna, Ranjana. *Dark Continents: Psychoanalysis and Colonialism*. Durham, N.C.: Duke University Press, 2003.

Labban, Mazen. "Deterritorializing Extraction: Bioaccumulation and the Planetary Mine." *Annals of the Association of American Geographers* 104, no. 3 (2014): 560–76.

Labban, Mazen. "Mine/ Machine," review of *Planetary Mine: Territories of Extraction under Late Capitalism,* by Martín Arboleda. *Dialogues in Human Geography* 12, no.1 (2022): 149–52.

Lake, Marilyn, and Henry Reynolds. *Drawing the Global Colour Line: White Men's Countries and the International Challenge of Racial Equality.* Cambridge: Cambridge University Press, 2008.

Lefebvre, Henri. *The Production of Space.* Translated by Donald Nicholson-Smith. Oxford: Blackwell, 1991.

Linebaugh, Peter, and Marcus Rediker. *The Many-Headed Hydra: Sailors, Slaves, Commoners, and the Hidden History of the Revolutionary Atlantic.* Boston: Beacon, 2000.

Manjapra, Kris. *Black Ghost of Empire: The Long Death of Slavery and the Failure of Emancipation.* New York: Simon & Schuster, 2022.

Marx, Karl. "Preface." In *A Contribution to the Critique of Political Economy.* Moscow: Progress, 1977. Online at Marxists.org.

Karl Marx, *Capital Volume III.* 1863–1883; repr. New York: International, 1999.

Mbembe, Achille. *Necropolitics.* Translated by Steven Corcoran. Durham, N.C.: Duke University Press, 2019.

Melville, Herman. *Moby-Dick.* 1851; repr. New York: Vintage, 2007.

Mezzadra, Sandro, and Brett Neilson. "On the Multiple Frontiers of Extraction: Excavating Contemporary Capitalism." *Cultural Studies* 31, no. 2–3 (2017): 185–204.

McKittrick, Katherine. *Dear Science and Other Stories.* Durham, N.C.: Duke University Press, 2021.

Morton, Adam David. "Traveling with Gramsci: The Spatiality of Passive Revolution." In *Gramsci: Space, Nature, Politics,* edited by Michael Ekers, Gillian Hart, Stefan Kipfer, and Alex Loftus, 47–64. London: John Wiley & Sons, 2013.

Moten, Fred. *In the Break: The Aesthetics of the Black Radical Tradition.* Minneapolis: University of Minnesota Press, 2003.

Moten, Fred and Stefano Harney. *The Undercommons: Fugitive Planning and Black Study.* Wivenhoe: Minor Compositions, 2013.

Nagahara, Yutuka *"Monsieur le capital* and *Madame la terre* Do Their Ghost-Dance: Globalization and the Nation-State." *South Atlantic Quarterly* 99, no. 4 (2000): 929–61.

Niemanis, Astrid "Held in Suspension: Mustard Gas Legalities in the Gotland Deep." In *Blue Legalities: The Life and Laws of the Sea,* edited by Irus Braverman and Elizabeth R. Johnson, 45–62. Durham, N.C.: Duke University Press, 2020.

Nightingale, Carl H. *Segregation: A Global History of Divided Cities*. Chicago: University of Chicago Press, 2012.

Ogle, Vanessa. "Archipelago Capitalism: Tax Havens, Offshore Money, and the State, 1950s–1970s." *American Historical Review*, December 2017, 1431–58.

Okiji, Fumi. *Jazz as Critique: Adorno and Black Expression Revisited*. Stanford, Calif.: Stanford University Press, 2018.

Ramaswamy, Sumathi. *The Lost Land of Lemuria: Fabulous Geographies, Catastrophic Histories*. Berkeley: University of California Press, 2004.

Ranganathan, Surabhi. "Ocean Floor Grab: International Law and the Making of an Extractive Imaginary." *European Journal of International Law* 30, no. 2 (2019): 573–600.

Ranganathan, Surabhi. "Decolonization and International Law: Putting the Ocean on the Map." *Journal of the History of International Law* 23 (2021): 161–83.

Rediker, Marcus. *Between the Devil and the Deep Blue Sea: Merchant Seamen, Pirates, and the Anglo-American Maritime World, 1700–1750*. Cambridge: Cambridge University Press, 1987.

Rediker, Marcus, *The Slave Ship: A Human History*. London: John Murray, 2007.

Rediker, Marcus. "History from below the Water Line: Sharks and the Atlantic Slave Trade." *Atlantic Studies* 5, no. 2 (2008): 285–297.

Rodenbiker, Jesse. "Urban Oceans: Social Differentiation in the City and the Sea." *Environment and Politics E: Nature and Space* 6, no. 1 (2022):412–32.

Rodney, Walter. *How Europe Underdeveloped Africa*, Washington, D.C.: Howard University Press, 1982.

Romero, Adam. *Economic Poisoning: Industrial Waste and the Chemicalization of American Agriculture*. Oakland: University of California Press, 2022.

Said, Edward. *The World, the Text, and the Critic*. Cambridge, Mass.: Harvard University Press, 1983.

Said, Edward. "On Critical Consciousness: Gramsci and Lukács." Edward Said Papers, Box 78, Folder 10. Rare Book and Manuscript Library, Columbia University, n.d.

Samuelson, Meg. "Thinking with Sharks: Racial Terror, Species Extinction and Other Anthropocene Fault Lines." *Australian Humanities Review* 63 (November 2018): 31–47.

Scott, Julius. *The Common Wind: Afro-American Currents in the Age of the Hatian Revolution*. London: Verso, 2018.

Shakur, Assata. *Assata: An Autobiography*. Chicago: Lawrence Hill, 1987.

Shutzer, Matthew. "Extractive Ecologies: Fossil Fuels, Global Capital, and the Political Economy of Development in India, 1870–1975." PhD diss., New York University, 2019.

Shutzer, Matthew. Review of *The Extractive Zone: Social Ecologies and Decolonial Perspectives,* by Macarena Gómez-Barris. *Enterprise and Society* 20, no.3 (2019): 741–43.

Shutzer, Matthew. "Subterranean Properties: India's Political Ecology of Coal, 1870–1975," *Comparative Studies in Society and History* 63, no. 2 (2021): 400–432.

Sivasundaram, Sujith. *Waves across the South: A New History of Revolution and Empire.* Chicago: University of Chicago Press, 2020.

Stephanie Smallwood. *Saltwater Slavery: A Middle Passage from Africa to American Diaspora,* Cambridge, Mass.: Harvard University Press, 2007.

Sugrue, Thomas. *The Origins of the Urban Crisis: Race and Inequality in Postwar Detroit.* Princeton, N.J.: Princeton University Press, 1996.

Thomas, Peter. "Gramsci's Revolutions." *Modern Intellectual History* 17, no. 1 (2020): 117–46.

Toscano, Alberto. "The World is Already without Us." *Social Text* 34, no. 2 (2016): 109–24.

Vine, David. *Island of Shame: The Secret History of the U.S. Military Base on Diego Garcia.* Princeton, N.J.: Princeton University Press, 2009.

Vine, David. *Base Nation: How U.S. Military Bases Abroad Harm America and the World.* New York: Metropolitan, 2015.

Wick, Alexis. *The Red Sea: In Search of Lost Space.* Oakland: University of California Press, 2016.

Wilderson, Frank. "Gramsci's Black Marx: Whither the Slave in Civil Society?" *Social Identities* 9, no. 2 (2003): 225–40.

Watts, Michael John. "Hyper-Extractivism and the Global Oil Assemblage: Visible and Invisible Networks in Frontier Spaces." In *Our Extractive Age: Expressions of Violence and Resistance,* edited by Judith Shapiro and John-Andrew McNeish, 207–48. London: Routledge, 2021.

(Continued from page iii)

Forerunners: Ideas First

Sharad Chari is associate professor in the Department of Geography and affiliate in Critical Theory, Rhetoric, and Gender and Women's Studies at the University of California, Berkeley; a member of the Marxist Institute for Research; research affiliate at the Wits Institute for Social and Economic Research, Johannesburg; and fellow at the Stellenbosch Institute of Adanced Studies. He is author of *Apartheid Remains* and *Fraternal Capital,* and co-editor of *Ethnographies of Power, Other Geographies,* and *The Development Reader*.